WHERE DO WE GO FROM HERE?

For my children, Michael and Katherine,
for whom a peaceful and charitable future
will mean so much

Timothy Kinahan

Where do we go from here?

PROTESTANTS AND THE FUTURE
OF NORTHERN IRELAND

the columba press

First edition, 1995, published by
the columba press
93 The Rise, Mount Merrion, Blackrock, Co Dublin

Cover by Bill Bolger
Origination by The Columba Press
Printed in Ireland by Genprint Ltd, Dublin

ISBN 1 85607 133 2

Acknowledgements

Much of Chapter 4 appeared in an earlier draft as an article in *Studies* (Spring 1987). The Papua New Guinea material appeared in an extended form in *Search* (Winter 1993). Biblical quotations are from the *Good News Version* except where otherwise stated.

Contents

Introduction 7

1 The Old Testament 11

2 The New Testament 26

3 Peace 44

4 Politics 51

5 Religion 72

Conclusion 91

Introduction

'I don't see how all this fits with Romans 13.'

It was the mid-1980s. We were in the middle of a residential conference, the subject of which was South Africa. The debate was challenging, and the direction radical. Some of the more conservative were feeling rather uncomfortable. Some of the questions raised were cutting very close to their Northern Irish bones.

Our speakers had been painting a vignette of South Africa, from the point of view of the South African Council of Churches. Active opposition to apartheid was stressed, and political action of various kinds was both described and proposed. Lobbying, boycotts, civil disobedience, solidarity with the oppressed, even violence, were all discussed, although not all were accepted. All very difficult for people who had been brought up to take St Paul's words in splendid isolation: 'Everyone must obey the state authorities, because no authority exists without God's permission, and the existing authorities were put there by God. Whoever opposes the existing authorities opposes what God has ordered; and anyone who does so will bring judgement on himself.' (Rom 13:1-2) Especially difficult for a Northern Irish Protestant like myself, who had been conditioned to regard all questions of justice as little more than a half truth, a political ploy used by the nationalist minority to massage discontent.

This book is a response to that situation. It is an attempt to relate seriously the biblical truths concerning the state, the *status quo*, and our relationships to them, to our own Northern Irish society, specifically from a Protestant point of view. I believe that, for too long, Northern Irish Protestant Christians like myself have let their politics rule their religion, rather than the other way round. Our so-called Protestantism has become so intimately bound up with our 'loyalism', our 'Britishness', that the two have become inseparable. In fact, the latter have begun to control the former to such an extent

7

that the true biblical witness is being ignored or (more often) read through orange-tinted spectacles.

However, I would not want it to be thought that I am being destructive: what I hope to achieve is a constructive critique from within. I am an Ulsterman, an Ulster Protestant, a member of the Church of Ireland, and I am proud of my heritage. I am proud of the contribution that my community has made over the years. I am proud of what we are and who we are, and it is on this basis that I wish to move forward.

Over the past decades my community has had a very bad press. This is partly because we have been quite abysmal at public relations, but it also because we have all too often taken attitudes that are neither endearing nor consonant with the faith and ideals that we as a community claim to hold. As an Ulsterman, I have felt the need to reflect on that.

The Northern Irish Protestant community is a disparate phenomenon. We are not homogenous. We come from Scottish, English and Irish stock. We are liberal and conservative, Calvinist and Arminian. We are rich and poor, good and bad – in short, a cross-section of the human race. But, as a mongrel brood, we do have much that unites us. We are, in part at least, a settler people and even those of us who trace our roots with pride back to ancient Celtic clans have taken on the mentality of our settler brothers and sisters. We are a proud and independent people, individualist and free, yet we are cut off from where we came from, and not entirely sure where we are or where we belong. For complicated historical reasons, we have thrown our political lot in with the British across the water, yet others find our Britishness peculiar, and we find it hard to trust our Irishness. As that legend in his own lifetime, Gusty Spence, once said: 'I'm British, but I'm Irish in my own peculiar way.'

Others look at us from outside and see, when they bother to look, an industrious people, a hard working folk. They see a people of great determination and inventiveness (such as Harry Ferguson), musical (such as James Galway and Sir Hamilton Harty), and artistic (such as Sir Tyrone Guthrie) and, although southerners, Jack Yeats and his poet brother William. They see writers and scholars like Helen Waddell, Louis MacNeice and C. S. Lewis. They see a people who did so much to mould the formative years of the United States of America, supplying no less than seven presidents to the young republic. They see a people who like to make their own decisions, and who do not take kindly to being ordered about, and who certainly do not like having their future decided by others, especially by others whom we perceive to be outsiders. And, although we are now almost synonymous with unionism, we are also a people who have played a major part in the nationalist movement – witness names such as Henry Joy McCracken, Wolf Tone, and Roger Casement. We have produced people like Bunting (who did more than anyone else to preserve the dying traditions of Irish traditional music) and many of the founding fathers of the Gaelic League.

Some of us find that hard to cope with. We like to think of ourselves as folk with a single creed. But that is a delusion. Part of our historic strength has been our very diversity, a diversity that we are in danger of throwing away. Part of the aim of this book is to encourage a pride in diversity, to encourage this community, which has in days gone by been so outward-looking and constructive, to look out with confidence once more, and to be itself with pride. I propose to do this by looking at the Bible, the source book for much of our culture and many of our turns of phrase, and seeking from within its pages some direction as to the way forward for us, a confident and outward-looking model.

So let us look at the biblical evidence. In Chapter 1, I shall limit myself to a study of the Old Testament attitudes to the *status quo*. Does the Bible tell us that, as Christians, we must always accept and support the powers that be? If not, what does it tell us? In Chapter 2, I attempt a similar treatment of the New Testament evidence, with an emphasis on trying to fathom the mind of Christ on these matters. Chapter 3, looks at the single issue of peace, and seeks to apply a Biblical understanding of the subject to our own situation in Northern Ireland.

In Chapters 4 and 5, I look specifically at political and religious questions raised by the foregoing analysis, seeking to challenge much of the prevailing orthodoxy with the Protestant/unionist community.

Much of my analysis centres round the concept of the *status quo*. I do this because, as I read it, the dominant ideology of my community is a conservative one, an attitude of mind that would prefer things not to change, that would cling to an irretrievable past. The

Shorter Oxford English Dictionary defines the *status quo* as 'The existing state of things', 'The state in which (things were) before (or are) now.' I seek to be constructively critical of the way things are now, and of the way things have been since the foundation of the Northern Irish State. I am not critical for criticism's sake, but rather because I seek to point out areas in which we, as a community, can profitably change direction, and advance with a new and more inclusive vision. We have a lot to offer. It would be a tragedy if, through fear, uncertainty or whatever, we squandered that opportunity. We have an inevitable part to play in the constructing of new relationships on this island. I believe that we need, as a community with its roots firmly in a biblical tradition, to play that part boldly, with imagination, and with faith. We need to be radical in all our ideas and relationships, not just because it is trendy to be radical, but because a genuine faith-inspired and biblically-grounded radicalism is the only way forward for those who would be true to their Lord and Master. We need to hammer out a new, inclusive vision in which all of us on this island can dare both to dream and reach the impossible, a consensus of opposites. We need to work for a land in which all of us, whatever our backgrounds, can feel free and proud to be ourselves. That is not beyond the reach of the Christian.

CHAPTER ONE

The Old Testament

1. The case for the *status quo*

There is much in the Old Testament to suggest that 'no authority exists without God's permission'. Perhaps this is clearest of all in the figure of David. Through the prophet Nathan God said to him 'I promise to keep you safe from all your enemies and to give you descendents, and I will make your kingdom last for ever. Your dynasty will never end.' (2 Sam 7:11, 16) God seems to be right behind David and the dynasty he founded. Indeed, the writer of the book of Chronicles simply ignores the whole history of the Northern Kingdom after it broke away from Judah in 931 BC on the basis that, since Jeroboam had rebelled against 'the Lord's annointed', neither he nor the people he represented were to be regarded as the chosen people of God. Because they had rebelled against the divinely appointed ruler, they had relinquished every claim that they might have had on the Lord or his blessings. 'Ever since then,' he writes, 'the people of the Northern Kingdom have been in rebellion against the dynasty of David.' (2 Chron 10:19) And with that, he cuts them off from recorded history. (cf. 2 Chron 13:12; Psalm 78: 67-69)

This whole 'Royal Theology' is especially noticeable in the book of Psalms, where it sometimes seems as though the Psalmists have become more royalist than the king himself. The covenant with David, instead of being conditional on the obedience of David and his sons (as it was in such Psalms as Ps 132:11-12), now seems absolute, without strings. Whatever they do, the kings of Judah will be defended and protected by the Lord Himself (Ps 89: 3-4, 30-37). Jerusalem, the city of David (2 Sam 5:9), which is intimately bound up with the whole theology of kingship in the Southern Kingdom of Judah (see Ps 48, for instance) is seen as impregnable (Pss 125:1-2; 48: 4-7; 48:12-14) and those who attack it as wicked fiends (Pss 129;

137:7-9). Examples could be multiplied from the Psalms, but rather than go through them all, can I just draw your attention to Psalms 2, 89 and 110?

This great emphasis on the divinely sanctioned monarchy is hardly surprising. The Psalms were, after all, written mostly for use in the Jerusalem temple, where the king himself would have worshipped. Some of them were perhaps sung at great ceremonial occasions (e.g. Ps 24), while others (such as Ps 45 and 72) were designed for royal weddings and coronations. We would no more expect these Psalms to be against the monarchy than we would expect Handel to have expressed republican sympathies in his Coronation Anthems!

But what of the rest of the Old Testament?

The laws of the Old Testament, although probably not collected in their present form until at least the eighth century BC, had long existed in an oral tradition that articulated the Israelites' own political self-awareness. These laws were regarded as divinely sanctioned (Ex 20:1: 'God spoke, and these were his words ...'), and disobedience against them was seen as an act of self-exclusion from the chosen people of God. (Ex 32:25-29; Lev 20:3-8; 26:14-39; Deut 6:15; 28:15-36; Josh 24:19-20; Ez 9:14 etc)

Although we can, with some justification, regard the Pentateuchal laws of the Old Testament as in some way the 'constitution' of early Israel, it would be unwise to think of any such *status quo* in formal modern terms. This was a largely illiterate people, not a bunch of lawyers. As with preliterate societies today, there is a very close identification between the people, the god(s) and the national/tribal ethos. This would not have been articulated, but rather assumed at a gut level. Overt rebellion against it was regarded as treachery, because the homogeneity and survival of the people in an unsettled and hostile world in large degree depended on it.

Ezra, who did so much to re-establish the Jewish people in their homeland after the exile, and who has rightly been called 'the father of Judaism', is a good example of a man who equated the Law of God with the *status quo*. He set up in Jerusalem a community whose touchstone of identity was the law (Neh 8:1-10; 39), codified and formalised in a manner that would have been totally strange to his ancestors. It was made fairly plain that disobedience either to the laws of the (Persian) empire, or to the laws of Moses was to be regarded with the utmost seriousness. In a document given to Ezra by the emperor Artaxerxes, we find the words 'if anyone disobeys the laws of your God or the laws of the empire, he is to be punished promptly; by death, or by exile, or by confiscation of his property, or by imprisonment.' (Ez 7:26) Ezra's response to this imperial *fiat* was to 'Praise the Lord' (v 27). Yet again, the *status quo* had received both secular and divine *imprimaturs*.

The book of Proverbs, a collection of wise sayings from various sources, is another case in point. The book is a fine embodiment of what scholars call the 'Wisdom Tradition', which stretched from the River Nile in Egypt to the River Euphrates in present day Iraq, an élite cosmopolitan way of thinking which in Israel was taken up with enthusiasm in educated circles. But, because it is the product of internationally minded and educated aristocrats, it naturally betrays a very conservative political outlook.

The emphasis here is on the right use of influence (e.g. 31:1-9), so that young men can be brought up to be 'honest, just and fair'. (1:3) Loyalty and faithfulness are much admired (3:3; 16:6; 20:28 etc); the aspiring man of influence is exhorted not to 'hesitate to rescue someone who is about to be executed unjustly' (24:11); and later in the same chapter he is told to 'have reverence for the Lord ... and honour the king. Have nothing to do with people who rebel against them.' (24:21) There is nothing particularly adventurous or radical here; indeed, this equation of rebellion against the Lord with rebellion against the king is conservatism writ large. The writers of Proverbs continually encourage their readers to virtue within the prevailing social structures, which themselves remain unchanged. Wealth, so often regarded elsewhere as the fruit of injustice (cf. Is 3:14-15; Amos 5:10ff), is here seen as a divine reward (Prov 3:10; 10:22; 13:21 etc.)

Perhaps we need to compare this with a passage such as Ecclesiastes 8:2-5: 'Do what the king says, and don't make any rash promises to God. The king can do whatever he likes, so depart from his presence; don't stay in such a dangerous place. The king acts with authority, and no one can challenge what he does. As long as you obey his commands, you are safe, and a wise man knows how and when to do it.' On the surface the writer of this passage seems to be saying that kings are a good thing to be obeyed, but a closer analysis of the tone of the whole book leads me to the feeling that he is writing with his tongue in his cheek. I am not at all sure that he actually intends us to take him all that seriously at this point. He is the sort of cynic who, with a nudge and a wink, wants us to know that his actual meaning is the direct opposite of what he seems to say on the surface. Although he is from the same social background as the writers of the rest of the Wisdom literature, and Proverbs in particular, he is not at one with them on this point. This does not say that he is actually disloyal – merely an uncommitted cynic.

With the prophets we move onto rather different ground. The 'Writing Prophets' of the Old Testament were not, so far as we can tell, institutional prophets in the manner of those who met Saul at Gibeah (1 Sam 10:10) or those who met Elijah and Elisha at Bethel and Jericho (1 Kgs 2:3, 5) although, as we shall see, there are some exceptions to this. They were, rather, men who had been called to be prophets in a highly individual manner, which paid scant regard to the normal procedures for appointing religious functionaries. Amos claimed that 'the Lord took me from my work as a shepherd and ordered me to come and prophesy to his people Israel.' (Amos 7:15) Isaiah, who seems to have been a man of some social standing and education, was called while at prayer in the temple. (Is 6) Jeremiah was marked as a prophet before he was born (Jer 1:5), and found frequent occasion to complain that he had had no choice in the matter. (Jer 12:1-6; 15:10-12; 20:7-18) By their very nature the prophets were individualists, a thorn in the flesh of the powers that be; they did not fit neatly into any pre-existing social or religious categories. But, despite that, they do not seem to have questioned the basic legitimacy of the existing social and political order. Even Amos, preaching in the Northern Kingdom (so summarily dismissed by the writer of Chronicles) accepts them as part of God's chosen people: 'Of all the nations on earth, you are the only one that I have known and cared for.' (Amos 3:2.)

This may sound surprising. Some may feel that the almost intemperate outbursts of the eighth-century Prophets (Amos, Hosea, Isaiah, Micah) are hardly supportive of the *status quo*. They prophesy doom and destruction on almost every page. Despite the superficial attractiveness of this line of argument, I do not think that it is tenable. Without going into a lengthy exegesis, which would be out of place in a volume of this scope, I would argue that the judgement they pronounce is on idolatry and the abuse of power and privilege. The sins are not attributed to the system, but to the whole nation, and especially the ruling classes within the nation. Punishment is for the whole nation, which will be defeated and sent into exile. (Amos 4:12; Hos 9:3-6; Mic 1:59; Is 10:14) The options put forward by these four prophets are basically two: either repent and change your ways (i.e. use the existing system properly), or be punished. There is no hint of a marxist or liberal analysis.

The same can basically be said of all the writing prophets. Nahum, although he exhibits an almost vitriolic hatred of the Assyrians (which is thoroughly understandable under the circumstances), does not refer to his own country at all. Zephaniah was himself of royal blood (Zeph 1:1), and although he has resounding criticisms of just about everybody else, stops short of actually criticising the king, the Lord's anointed, in person (Zeph 1:8). Habakkuk, who was probably an official prophet, throws serious questions at God about the prevailing state of things. (Hab 1:2-4) Yet he does not attempt to alter structures. Instead, he is content to 'wait quietly for the time to come when God will punish those who attack us.' (Hab 3:16)

Jeremiah, the greatest of all the pre-exilic prophets, is a rather more complex character. Yet he, like Isaiah before him, seems to have served as an unofficial foreign policy advisor to the king of the day. (Jer 2:18; 27:8-11; 38:17-18) No doubt he was unconventional, and frequently unpopular (11:21-23; 26:1-24; 32:3; 36:26; 38:1-6); yet, despite it all he can still see hope in the system, purified and restored (30:8-9). Like all his predecessors he works for a radical improvement and purification of existing structures and theologies, not for the total overthrow and replacement of the system. For the system, most notably in its Davidic heart, is a gift of God, and therefore sacrosanct.

The exilic and post-exilic prophets are not markedly different in their emphases. Second Isaiah (the name generally given to the author of Isaiah chapters 40-55, who was writing during the time of the exile, about 540 BC) and Ezekiel (who was preaching about forty years earlier) have at the core of their preaching a message of restoration: Israel will be returned to Jerusalem (Is 55:7-12; Ezek 36:24) where the religious cult will be revitalised (Is 41:16; Ezek 40:1-48; 35) and where the Lord's people will be able to live under the law of the Lord and receive the blessings promised to David. (Is

55:3; Ezek 37:15-28) Haggai and Zechariah, who were working at
the time the temple was being rebuilt (c. 520 BC), both preached
messages of encouragement to those who were doing the rebuild-
ing work. Both believed that the troubles within the Persian empire
were signs of the imminent breakthrough of God's kingdom. (Hag
2:20-23; Zech 1:18-21) Malachi is not concerned with the immediate
political situation in which he found himself; so much so that scholars are divided as to when he actually did preach!

Yet all these exilic and post-exilic men are real signs that the Old
Testament is not a political treatise, let alone monochrome in its
political viewpoint. They are a diverse lot, occasionally very radical, yet at bottom rather more conservative and traditional. But they
are conservative only insofar as they are supporters of the *status quo
ante*: in other words, they hark back to the golden Davidic age, and
seek the restoration of Israel to that pristine and pure ideal. To all of
them, the present situation is far from ideal: to the prophets of the
exile the *status quo*, in which they are living in exile under an idolatrous régime, is important only insofar as it is to be overthrown by
God. The Prophets who preached after the exile are united in their
realisation that the situation under which they are living is not perfect. They likewise look to the Davidic model, with its structures
and its promises. They are only supporters of existing structures
where they can fairly be said to reflect the will of God and promote
the greater good of his people Israel.

This observation encourages me to retrace my steps and look at
the Old Testament from a different point of view. How far does it
encourage those who would like to rebel against, or at least actively
oppose, the existing structures of society and of the state ?

2. The case against the *status quo*

The roots of any reaction against the *status quo* within Israel can be
found in the laws of the Old Testament where, amongst the often
obscure and archaic laws whose relevance escapes us today, there
are many strong prescriptions in favour of respecting the old (Lev
19:32); being kind to foreigners (Lev 23:33; Ex 22:25; Deut 24:17ff);
not cheating (Lev 25:35; Deut 25:13-15); refusing bribes (Deut 16:19),
and justice and fairness between Israelites (Ex 22 *et passim*). These
are the laws, the covenant, to which (as we shall see) the prophets
kept referring. These were the ideal for which Israel strived, and

which she usually failed to achieve. Insofar as the *status quo* did not reflect these ideals, it was bringing judgement upon itself: it can be argued (e.g. by St Paul in Rom 3) that the laws of the Old Testament posited such a high standard that no society could hope to live up to it. Amongst the religiously insistent, constructive opposition became the norm.

The Jubilee is a fine example of this naïve political idealism within the Old Testament laws. It stipulated that every fiftieth year 'all property that has been sold shall be restored to the original owner or his descendents, and anyone who has been sold as a slave shall be returned to his family.' (Lev 25:10) No fields were to be cultivated, and the year was to be one long sabbath, a celebration of freedom and the generosity of God. This is extreme: had Israel obeyed it, there would have been no long-term inequality of wealth distribution, no injustice and no oppression. It is almost a built-in criticism of any and every human society, one that can always be used by idealists to hammer the powers that be. Had it ever been taken seriously its revolutionary impact would have turned Israelite society upside-down.

There were also safety valves in Israelite society, such as the nabi and the Nazirites, which allowed for eccentricity and rebelliousness to be channelled in socially acceptable directions. Both the nabi and the Nazirites were standing rebukes to the powerful and the rich: the nabi were the cult prophets who were attached to shrines around the country, and whose wild behaviour was frequently a cause for comment (e.g. 1 Sam 10:10; 2 Kgs 2:1-18). The Nazirites were an outrageous bunch, not allowed to drink wine (Num 6:4) or cut their hair (Num 6:5), bound by a vow of limited duration. These both seem to have been, amongst other things, a socially acceptable way of saying 'I object to the values of society', a kind of formalised drop-out.

So we can see that the ideals of early Israel, if kept strictly in focus, would have been a constant irritant to those in power. She also had means of dealing with socially unacceptable behaviour, even rebelliousness. Within this context, the Exodus is the first and perhaps the most obvious example of rebellion against established authority. The people of Israel were slaves in Egypt (Ex 1), who seem to have had little hope of liberation until Moses was called by God: 'I have seen how cruelly my people are treated in Egypt; I have heard them cry out to be rescued from their slave drivers. I know all about their suffering, and so I have come down to rescue them ... Now I am sending you to the king of Egypt so that you can lead my people out of his country.' (Ex 3:7-10) The king (Pharoah) refuses, and after a long psychological war he is finally defied and defeated at the Red Sea (Ex 14). The Exodus is, arguably, the first recorded case of a just revolution with strong theological undertones.

The period of the Judges also shows us the Lord God repeatedly upsetting the political norms of the day. Sometimes he does this in order to punish the people of Israel, as when he allows them to be conquered by Jabin (Jdgs 4:2) or the Midianities (Jdgs 6:1). At other times he does it in order to liberate his people from their oppressive punishment. One and all the Judges are sent by God to free them from their oppressors (e.g. Jdgs 3:9; 3:15; 4:4-7; 6:7-14 etc); indeed, the formula 'The people of Israel sinned against the Lord', followed by oppression by an outside power, a cry for help to the Lord, and a final liberation by a divinely appointed judge is recurrent throughout the whole book. It seems that the Lord is no defender of established régimes that displease him. Yet, it is hard to avoid the impression that the judges (and everyone else in the drama) are no more than pawns in a divine game, appointed or chosen for their various rôles. It is hard to argue in favour of just revolution from their examples.

It is perhaps not surprising that David should, once again, give us food for thought. He was, after all, a rebel who skilfully manipulated those forces that were opposed to King Saul, and who inherited the crown on the death of Saul. He was anointed king by the priest Samuel (1 Sam 16), who was acting on the direct orders of the Lord himself. Previously Saul had been cast aside in a dramatic incident: 'Then Samuel turned to leave, but Saul caught hold of his cloak and it tore. Samuel said to him, "The Lord has torn the kingdom of Israel away from you this day and given it to someone who is a better man than you."' (1 Sam 15:27-28) David may have been the Lord's anointed, chosen by God to play the rôle he did: but he comes out of the narrative in 1 and 2 Samuel as a man of flesh and blood, of doubt and hope and fear, very conscious of what he was doing. As a result, his example is of far greater interest to us.

David is very cautious about rebellion. When he has Saul in his grasp, he refuses to harm him: 'May the Lord keep me from doing any harm to my master, whom the Lord chose as king ! I must not harm him in the least, because he is the king chosen by the Lord.' (1 Sam 24:6) A little later he has another opportunity to dispose of his rival, but again he lets the chance slip, for much the same reasons: 'You must not harm him! The Lord will certainly punish whoever harms his chosen king.' (1 Sam 26:9) It could be argued that David is being politically very astute, for by showing mercy, and then theologising that mercy, he was no doubt laying the foundations of his support for the future. Saul was very definitely unbalanced by this time, and David could easily have justified the overthrow of an unbalanced king, yet his action in not overthrowing him would have won him a great deal of sympathy. But he was still a rebel.

There are plenty of other examples of divinely sanctioned rebellion. On the death of Solomon, Jeroboam the son of Nebat rebelled against his successor Rehoboam, having previously been given the go ahead to do so by the prophet Ahijah: 'Ahijah took off the new robe he was wearing, tore it into twelve pieces, and said to Jeroboam, "Take ten pieces for yourself, because the Lord, the God of Israel, says to you, I am going to take the kingdom away from Solomon, and will give you ten tribes."' (1 Kgs 11:30-31) The writer of Chronicles does not even mention this event!

In the wisdom literature there is, as we would expect, little to encourage us to disapprove of the powers that be. The only book to offer anything in this line is Ecclesiastes. We have already seen how, in Chapter 8, he refers tongue-in-cheek to kings. He is even more unconventional in 3:16-4:16, where he refers to the oppressors who 'have power on their side'. (Eccl 4:1) He puts large question marks over the whole concept of political power and its relationship to the injustice and stupidity of the world. Yet to call him a witness in favour of rebellion is a bit far fetched: it would be more accurate to class him among the dissatisfied, but one of the dissatisfied who is unsure exactly what to do about his dissatisfaction!

Elijah is perhaps the most overtly political of the Old Testament prophets. His main quarrel was not so much with the monarchy or the ruling classes as such, but with the religious policies followed by them. Yet the rebellion is clear enough. He is commanded to go and anoint 'Jehu the son of Nimshi as king of Israel' (1 Kgs 19:16), and at a later stage condemns the king (Ahab) in no uncertain terms: 'You have devoted yourself completely to doing what is wrong in the Lord's sight. So the Lord says to you, "I will bring disaster on you."' The disaster does come, but not through open armed rebellion. Ahab dies in the course of one of his foreign wars, and is succeeded by his son Ahaziah (1 Kgs 22:51). Elijah's opposition was severe, but it did not extend to the violent overthrow of the régime. His path was the path of a Ghandi or a Luther King, the path of unarmed resistance, of non-violent opposition. In the context of his time, that was a fairly unusual path. (The murder of the prophets of Baal is a notable exception to this.) Yet, however it is interpreted, it is hard to see Elijah as a loyal subject! He is a complex character, not always consistent in his methods. His is probably the best case study in religio-political opposition in the whole of the Old Testament.

At a later date, Jehu is anointed king, although not by Elijah. We do not know the name of the man who did it, but the event is recorded graphically for us: 'The young prophet poured the olive oil on Jehu's head and said to him, "The Lord, the God of Israel, proclaims, I anoint you the king of my people Israel. You are to kill your master the king, that son of Ahab..." After saying this, the young prophet left the room and fled.' (2 Kgs 9:6-10) Regicide is here not merely condoned, but actually enjoined, although about a century later this self same murder is condemned by Hosea (Hos 1:4).

As we have seen earlier in this chapter, it can certainly be argued that the eighth-century prophets, and their successors, were no friends of the powers that be. However, this does not seem to have implied that they were either social or political revolutionaries in any modern sense of the term. Rather, they were repeatedly trying to encourage the people, in extreme language, to return to the original idea of the *status quo*, as epitomised by the covenant. As far as the prophets were concerned, this covenant contained within itself all the necessary legislation and ideas for a perfect society. Its provisions of justice for widows and orphans, its provisions against exploitation of the powerless, and above all its stipulation of the jubilee (by which all property was to be returned to its original owners, and all slaves freed, every fifty years), were seen as guarantees sufficient to ensure a well-balanced and just society. Modern sociologists may feel inclined to argue that the covenant was not really a practical option in the changed circumstances of the settled kingdom. Most of its provisions were laid down at a time when Israel was an agrarian or even nomadic people, and were therefore incompatible with the developed structures of the monarchy and a settled population. Given that, it is argued, it is hardly surprising that the prophets seem to have been talking to deaf ears for so long.

Of course, we cannot expect the prophets to have thought along these lines. Again and again they encourage the people to be faithful to the covenant. Jeremiah is told to 'go to the cities of Judah and to the streets of Jerusalem. Proclaim my message there, and tell the people to listen to the terms of the covenant and to obey them.' (Jer 11:6) ... 'it is the same covenant I made with their ancestors when I brought them out of Egypt' (ibid v 4). This could be said to be the guiding theme of all the writing prophets: the call to 'return to the Lord your God' (Hos 14:1; Mal 3:7, etc.). It is expressed in many different ways, and with varying degrees of forcefulness, but it is always there.

Much of the prophetic wrath is aimed at the people's idolatry – the laws of the Pentateuch are very strict on the matter – and it is, along with questions of justice, the main concern of the prophetic witness. The basic commands are 'Worship no God but me' and 'Do not make for yourselves images of anything in heaven or on earth or under the earth. Do not bow down to any idol.' (Ex 20:3-5) Whenever these commands were broken, the punishment upon Israel was severe: three thousand died as a result of the Golden Calf incident at the foot of Sinai (Ex 32:28). Elijah's main concern was to counter the influence of Baal worship that was being introduced by Jezebel, the Tyrian wife of King Ahab (1 Kgs 16:29ff), even to the extent of killing four hundred and fifty of the prophets of Baal (1 Kgs 18). The writer of the two books of Kings judges all rulers on the basis of their faithfulness to the strict monotheism of Exodus 20 (e.g. 1 Kgs 16:13; 2 Kgs 12:2-3; 13:2,11; 14:3-4, etc.). Amos, amidst all his despairing cries for justice, also attacks idolatry: 'They have despised my teachings and have not kept my commands. They have been led astray by the same false Gods that their ancestors served...' (Amos 2:4) Hosea's whole life was a parable of Israel's 'harlotry'. Isaiah begins his prophesy by saying 'You have rejected the Lord, the holy God of Israel, and have turned your backs on him.' (Is 1:4) And his successor prophet, preaching in Babylon during the exile, is merciless in his attacks on idol worship: 'the idol he holds in his hand is not a god at all'. (Is 44:20; cf Ps 115)

It is not necessary to go into more detail here, save to point out that the condemnation of idolatry is every bit as strong as the condemnation of injustice: the two are intimately related. Social justice (i.e. a right relationship with our neighbour) is a necessary consequence of a right relationship with God. Therefore idolatry is every bit as much an indictable offence as injustice. So the prophets condemn it, and support those who oppose it.

Yet all this is only revolutionary in that it calls for a radical change in the way that the system is operated – a return to roots. The prophets do not mince their words: 'The city that once was faithful is behaving like a whore ... your leaders are rebels and friends of thieves; they are always accepting gifts and bribes.' (Is 1:21-23); 'Even if Moses and Samuel were standing here pleading with me, I would not show these people any mercy.' (Jer 15:1); 'You are like a rotten and worthless vine.' (Jer 2:21); Ezekiel likens Israel to a prostitute who 'was filled with lust for oversexed men who had all the lustfulness of donkeys or stallions.' (Ezek 23:20); Hosea is asked to 'plead with her to stop her adultery and prostitution.' (Hos 2:2); Amos likens the women of Samaria to the 'well fed cows of Bashan' (Amos 4:1). The list is endless: their violent language is designed to shock the people out of their apathy, to force them to read the 'signs of the times' aright; it is designed to get the people to return to the Lord, and live honestly and obediently under the law. Failing that, the system will be ended.

Despite all this, none of the writing prophets seem to countenance civil disobedience, of the sort toyed with by Elijah. The call for the ending of the system is not for an internally generated revolution. That comes from outside, from Assyria (Amos 6:14; Is 8:7) or Babylon (Jer 25:9; Ezek 12:13). There is no call for the people to rise up and change the power structures for themselves, or for them to rise up against the oppressive ruling classes. The prophets one and all suggest that, when the punishment does come, and the people have served their time in exile, a 'remnant' will return to start anew (Is 10:21; Mic 5:3; Jer 23:3, etc.). Yet even this new start is envisaged in terms of a Davidic monarchy, the Mosaic law, and the covenant implications that those imply. The system itself is not criticised, only the operation of that system, and the human abuses of it. The system itself seems to have been regarded, implicitly or explicitly, as a gift of God, as fundamentally good, and therefore not to be challenged. We may look to the writing prophets of the Old Testament for support in our cries for social justice, but not if we want support for our campaigns of civil disobedience or revolution. They were reformers, radical in the sense that they wanted to 'return to roots'. They were not liberation theologians.

Even so, there are some very definite criticisms of the prevailing 'Royal Theology' in the prophetic corpus. At one level the criticisms are aimed not at the theology itself, but at the false confidence placed *in* that theology. Both Micah and Jeremiah, for instance, attack those who repeat blindly such words as 'the Lord is with us' (Mic 3:11) or 'We are safe! This is the Lord's temple, this is the Lord's temple, this is the Lord's temple.' (Jer 7:4) This kind of blind trust was obviously very far from the ideal posited by the prophets. But their attitude to it contains within itself hints of a more total rejection of the whole monarchy, such as we see in the contemporary writer of parts of 1 Samuel. This writer regarded the desire for an earthly king as a rejection of the kingship of the Lord God himself (1 Sam 8:10-22; 12:19). Hosea is very explicit: 'In my anger I have given you kings, and in my fury I have taken them away' (Hos 13:11).

The concept of the Messiah. which we will look at in a little more detail when we see what use Jesus made of the title, is a little ambiguous for the point of view of our study. For a start, the word itself is rarely used in the Old Testament, only really gaining a major significance in the intertestamental period. On the one hand, it is a Davidic Messiah to whom the people look forward (Ezek 34:23f; 37:24f; Hos 3:5; Zech 12:7-14), while on the other hand, the very apocalyptic context in which the Messianic expectations grew up was one in which many people were despairing of this world, and looking for the irruption of God to end it, and to start anew. History had ceased to hold any attraction for the persecuted Jews, so they looked to a hope that lay beyond the limitations of that history. The Messiah, in his Davidic garb, was to come to end all *status quos*, all powers that be, and replace them with a new age, in which the Kingdom of God would be with men. This sort of thinking is almost an abandonment of the political process.

Now let us try to draw some conclusions from the very diverse evidence of the Old Testament. Its very diversity must lead us to withhold judgement on the matter in question. There is no united voice as to whether men should be supporters of the *status quo* or against it. The dominant voice is one of support, tinged with criticism; yet at times that criticism is so violent that it can hardly be called supportive at all.

This diversity should not dismay us. The Old Testament is a complex book which records (amongst other things) the acts and words of men over a wide period of time. Its complexity takes account of the complexity of the human condition: indeed, it reflects that very complexity. No attempt is made to push us in one direction, to say 'This is the only valid opinion on the matter'. We are left with the dignity of being able to make up our own minds. Were kings a good idea? We are free to follow the earlier of the two main sources in 1 Samuel, and Micah, and say that they were not; but are equally free to regard them as God's gift to the people of Israel, following many of the psalms. Was Jehu right to rebel against Ahab's dynasty? We are free to say 'Yes' with the writer of Kings, or 'No' with Hosea. Likewise today: there is no simple blueprint for us to follow. We have to assess the situation for ourselves, and make our own decisions on the basis of that assessment. We are given some criteria to help us in that process (such as justice, and the extent to which any particular situation reflects the will of God) but ultimately the decision rests with us, our intellects and our conscience.

Although the Old Testament rarely criticises the *status quo* per se, it persistently challenges the misuse of power by those who wield it. The prophets, even those closest to the Royal court, were a continual abrasive to those with wealth and authority, a model of constructive opposition. But there is no doubt that the Old Testament does go further on occasions and countenance the violent overthrow of a rotten régime.

In this brief overview of the Old Testament evidence, I have deliberately looked only at the evidence in relation to Israel and Judah, and have ignored the repeated denunciations and promises of destruction for foreign nations, which make up a significant proportion of the prophetic *corpus*. Foreign nations are generally regarded as evil and idolatrous, deserving only of punishment. They are seen from a very xenophobic standpoint. It is easy to condemn the outsider. I have thought it more important to stay at home.

Even though I have argued for the view that the basic prophetic plea is for a return to the *status quo ante*, I do not believe that we can just transfer that line of argument to our own situation in Northern Ireland today. The most we can do is take the prophetic way of thinking and apply it to our own unique situation, as a formative basis for our own thinking. We cannot just transfer conclusions from the seventh century BC to our own day. If we were to do that, and take the prophetic arguments simplistically to their logical conclusion, we would have to work for the overthrow of all existing systems and régimes, insofar as they all fail to live up to the Mosaic/Davidic ideal.

That would seem to be the key to an adequate understanding of the political stance of the Old Testament writers. They have an ideal, symbolised by the covenant (however conceptualised), and judge all existing systems in relation to it. If they fall short, then they are in for judgement in varying degrees. In that all our existing political systems fall short of the ideals of justice, equality and monolatry symbolised by those covenants, all are harshly judged. All, if they fail to reform themselves from within, are liable for destruction from without, and occasionally for revolution from within. The Old Testament, despite its conflicting witnesses, offers no comfort to those who would like to maintain the *status quo*, in Northern Ireland or anywhere else. It also offers no comfort to those in Northern Ireland who blindly repeat the slogans of 'majority rule' and 'democracy'. Neither does it offer any simple blueprint for those who would like to overthrow the present system, and replace it with something different. It calls us, rather, into a critical relationship with all political systems and ideals. This calls for maturity, and a willingness to accept diversity. Neither the Old Testament world, nor our world today, are as simple as some people would like them to be!

CHAPTER 2

The New Testament

'Taking it all in all, the New Testament is stony ground for those who are seeking a gospel of social revolution or even of social reform. They would find more to encourage them in the pages of the Old Testament.' (A. T. Hanson, *Search* viii: 2 p 68)

'This revolutionary commitment has made us discover the liberating work of Christ.' (Final document of the Santiago conference 'Christians for socialism', quoted in Bonino, *Revolutionary Theology comes of Age*, p xxiv)

The New Testament is the product of the early church, and as such naturally reflects the concerns of that church. This is most obvious in the epistles, but is also noticeable in the gospels themselves, in which the person of Jesus, and his message, are to some extent overlaid by the kerygmatic purposes of the evangelists. As a result, there is a healthy tension within the New Testament both in political matters and in more doctrinal ones. Both Hanson, from his position within the Western European liberal/conservative establishment, and the Christian socialists of the Santiago conference quoted above, from their position within the new Latin American liberationalist establishment, have tended to underplay this tension in pursuit of the respective over-simplifications.

The gospel portrait of Jesus is obviously central to any Christian thinking, be it ethical, political, social or theological. It is not possible to reconstruct a 'historical' Jesus; the 150-odd pages of the gospels can hardly be called exhaustive; they were written approximately 1900 years ago; they were never intended as biographies in the modern sense of that term; and ever since they were written men and women have tended to look to them for confirmation of their own prejudices. The gospels have been used as proof texts by

both revolutionaries and oppressive establishments, by both marx-
ists and neo-fascists. None of us come to them with clear minds,
without preconceived notions; each of us knows what we want to
find there and as a result we are all too often blinded to the startling
originality of the Jesus who is revealed there. These are also *my*
problems, and not just the problems of those who will disagree
with me! However, aware of these dangers, I approach the gospels
as I approached the Old Testament: in the hope that I can unearth
from through the centuries the meaning that was intended by the
original writers.

The first thing that we can safely say is that Jesus is not primarily
concerned with politics or with the powers that be. When his
opponents tried to trap him with the question 'Is it against our Law
to pay taxes to the Roman Emperor or not ?' (Mt 22:17), he chose
cleverly to parry their question by giving them the answer 'Well
then, pay to the emperor what belongs to the emperor, and pay to
God what belongs to God.' (Mt 22:21) He avoids their trap: his
opponents cannot now accuse him of disloyalty either to the Jewish
Law, or to the Roman emperor. Jesus was not there to get sucked
into their party political feuds.

Furthermore, he was not concerned with the assumption of
political power in any form. Repeatedly, throughout his ministry,
we see him being tempted by it, and resisting that temptation as
diabolical. Right at the start of his preaching ministry, he goes out
into the desert. There he is tempted by the devil who shows him 'all
the kingdoms of the world in all their greatness.' 'All this I will give
you,' the devil says, 'if you will kneel down and worship me.' (Mt
4:8-9) Jesus refuses. Political power was not his way.

Later on, Jesus is recognised as the Messiah by Peter (Mk 8:29),
and immediately orders the disciples not to tell anyone about it. As
we saw briefly in the last chapter, the concept of the Messiah in the
Old Testament was highly political and the political element in it
had been deepened and exaggerated in the period in between the
Testaments, so that by the time of Christ it had become political
dynamite. In the Psalms of Solomon, many of which were probably
written only shortly before the birth of Jesus, the Messiah is por-
trayed as one who will come to remove the heathen from Jerusalem
and purge the godless (17:21-25) and establish an exclusive kingdom of pure and holy people. (17:26-29) The writer of 2 Esdras,

writing perhaps a little earlier, sees him as a great leader who will inaugurate a period of 400 years of happiness, but not before he has destroyed all the godless (2 Esdras 7:26-44). The pious Jew who, until AD 70, prayed at the end of every Passover meal for redemption from the occupying power of Rome, would no doubt have been thinking along similar lines.

Jesus did not look at his messiahship in these terms at all. He explains that, as 'Son of Man' (in Mt 16:21 he says 'I'), he must 'suffer much and be rejected by the elders, the chief priests, and the teachers of the Law. He will be put to death, but three days later will rise to life' (Mk 8:31). Notice how immediately he moves away from the word Messiah, with all its political overtones, and introduces instead the cryptic concept 'Son of Man'. He tries to explain the work of the Messiah in terms that Peter was not, at that stage, either ready or willing to understand. Presumably Peter had visions of the Messiah inaugurating an era of political independence, purity and peace. When he rebukes Jesus, trying to persuade him away from this chosen path, he gets a flea in the ear: 'Get away from me, Satan. Your thoughts don't come from God, but from man!' (Mk 8:33) These words are a very close echo of those used to Satan himself in the wilderness (Mt 4:10).

It is obvious from this that political power was an attractive option to Jesus. It would have conveniently short-cut the way to the Kingdom of God, or at least appeared to do so. Yet Jesus regards it as a satanic temptation. Throughout his ministry he goes out of his way to dispel any thoughts that he was the Messiah, because of the political hopes it would have raised in people's consciousness. Where the people believed that the Messiah was to be a 'Son of David', Jesus asks 'How can the Messiah be David's son?' (Mk 12:37) When the pharisees come and specifically ask for proof signs (such as were expected of the Messiah), Jesus replies, 'Why do the people of this day ask for a miracle? No, I tell you! No such proof will be given to these people!' (Mk 8:12) While the teachers of the Law said that Elijah must come first, he replied, 'Elijah must indeed come first in order to get everything ready. Yet why do the scriptures say that the Son of Man will suffer much and be rejected? I tell you, however, that Elijah has already come and that people treated him just as they pleased.' (Mk 9:12f) While the teachers of the Law looked for a fulfilment of the messianic mission during the lifetime of the Messiah, Jesus is crucified and dies, for all the world to see, a failure.

Jesus does not simply reject the title Messiah. Rather, he injects into it a new content that would have made it totally unrecognisable to his fellow Jews, just as it was to Peter. It is hardly surprising that they were confused: on some occasions he does accept the title 'Son of David' (e.g. Mt 21:9); for most of his ministry he does perform signs and wonders, which were seen as messianic pointers by many of those who followed him (e.g. Jn 6:14); when John the Baptist's messengers asked him whether he was 'the one he said was going to come' (Lk 7:20), Jesus replies with a resounding 'Yes' by referring back to Old Testament prophesy (Is 35:56; 61:1): 'Go back and tell John what you have seen and heard: the blind can see, the lame can walk, the lepers are cleansed, the deaf can hear, the dead are raised to life, and the good news is preached to the poor.' (Lk 7:22) In other words, the signs of the messianic kingdom are already here! On the one hand, he encourages messianic expectations, and on the other he does all he can to dampen them. He does not reject the title outright: he re-interprets it. In his life and witness it becomes almost unrecognisable. The political, power-centred content is thrown away. Instead Jesus emphasises suffering (see Mt 17:12), service (see Jn 13:2-17) and the new values of the Kingdom of God (Mt 5:1-6:34).

This is apparent throughout the gospels. At the triumphant entry into Jerusalem Jesus could well have turned the fervour of the crowd to a revolutionary purpose (Mt 21:1-11; Mk 11:1-11; Lk 19:28-40; John 12:12-19). Instead, he embarked on a course of action that so alienated them that, a few days later, they were shouting for his execution (Mt 27:22-25; Mk 15:11-15; Lk 23:18-25; Jn 19:6-16). After the feeding of the five thousand, Jesus senses 'that they were about to come and sieze him in order to make him king by force; so he went off to the hills by himself.' (Jn 6:15) In short, Jesus chose to submit himself voluntarily to the forces of evil, rather than use the levers of power against them.

This pinpoints Jesus as unwilling to get involved in the power structures of his day, on either side. He was not willing to give support to either the Romans (who were occupying his country), or to the zealots (who were trying to expel the Romans by waging a spasmodic and largely ineffectual guerilla war). His little band of twelve disciples was chosen, in part, to reveal how, in the Kingdom of God, these loyalties are transcended. Amongst his disciples were representatives of both extreme parties: Simon was a zealot (Mk 3:18; Lk 6:15) and Levi a tax-collector (Mt 9:9-11; Lk 5:27-30; Mk 2:13-17), and as such one of the despised collaborator class. We have no evidence that either of them changed their political points of view, although we can assume that Simon abandoned his support for violence, and Levi his corruption. Yet, whether they changed or not, they both remained loyal followers of Jesus who, if legend is to be believed, both died martyrs' deaths, Simon in Persia and Levi in Ethiopia. The Kingdom of God transcended their political allegiances and was not, in itself, concerned with the structures of society, or the nature of government.

Yet Jesus does take sides. He can be extremely rude about both the political and religious authorities, referring to Herod as 'that fox' (Lk 13:32) and to the Pharisees as hypocrites (Mt 23:13), blind guides (Mt 23:16), fools (Mt 23:17), whitewashed tombs (Mt 23:27); as well as criticising them for not practicing what they preached (Mt 23:5-12). He is most certainly not in favour of the behaviour of the rich and powerful. But that is not to say that he rejects them as people: he was just as willing to eat with an influential pharisee (Lk 7:36ff) as he was to eat with 'publicans and sinners'. (Mt 11:19) Our Lord's interest lay with people: he sought to change them. It just so happens that it is the rich and powerful that are generally in greater need of change.

Now, the early church found itself in a rather different position. While Jesus had expected the imminent end of the age (e.g. Mt 10:23; Mk 9:1; Lk 10:22-37; Jn 21:22) and had therefore a less immediate interest in the temporal questions that bothered his contemporaries, the early church very soon had to work out how it was to relate to the authorities, just as the authorities had to decide what to do about them. We see this process at work in the rest of the New Testament.

St Paul met with a good deal of persecution, from 'the Jews' (Acts 13:50; 17:5,13; 18:12f; 2 Cor 11:26; 1 Thess 2:14-15), from frenzied mobs (Acts 14:19; 19:21ff; 21:31; 2 Cor 11:25), and from the authorities, both Jewish (Acts 22:30; 23:15; 2 Cor 11:24) and Roman (Acts 16:22; 24:27; 2 Cor 11:25), yet he never once expresses any bitterness against his persecutors, nor does he ever suggest that their tenure of office is rendered invalid by their behaviour. We have seen how he wrote to the Romans, 'Everyone must obey the state authorities, because no authority exists without God's permission, and the existing authorities have been put there by God. Whoever opposes the existing authorities opposes what God has ordered; and anyone who does so will bring judgement on himself.' (Rom 13:1-2) 'For we are not fighting against human beings, but against wicked spiritual forces in the heavenly world, the rulers, authorities and powers of this dark age.' (Eph 6:12) Paul shows an almost amazing lack of interest in the social and political context in which he was working. He gets on with the job of evangelising and nurturing the communities which he has evangelised, treating his troubles as opportunities, and not as causes for complaint. Paul saw himself as fighting a spiritual battle, not a worldly one.

We should make two points at this stage of our argument. Firstly, just because Paul says that we should obey the state authorities, does not mean that he was an active supporter of those same authorities. Secondly, Paul was an evangelist, with his own specific concerns; we cannot therefore say that, just because Paul accepted the *status quo*, perhaps reluctantly, that we in our different situations with our different rôles in church and society must necessarily take the same attitude as he did.

Maybe Paul's attitude should not surprise us. The early church was a tiny and rather suspect community, as the book of Acts makes abundantly clear. One of the first references that we have to Christians outside the New Testament confirms this. In about the year AD 111, the younger Pliny was appointed imperial legate in the Roman Province of Bithynia. He soon came up against the Christians, and it seems that by then it was already considered a crime even to profess the name of Christ. In one of his letters to the emperor Trajan he wrote:

> So far this has been my procedure when people were charged before me with being Christians. I have asked the accused themselves if they were Christians; if they said 'Yes', I asked them a second time and a third time, warning them of the penalty; if they persisted, I led them off to execution. (Pliny Ep x 96)

A very similar procedure is recorded to have taken place in the year 155, in Smyrna, at the 'trial' and execution of Bishop Polycarp. Under these circumstances it would have been impractical to have entertained thoughts of revolution. The Roman Empire was almost unbelievably powerful, while the Christians were a very small, scattered, and beleaguered group. The Roman *status quo* may not have been appreciated, but it was accepted as part of 'this world' that was soon to be overthrown by the final intervention of God.

This attitude underlies all the rest of the New Testament. The author of 1 Peter appeals to his readers:

> Your conduct among the heathen should be so good that when they accuse you of being evil doers they will have to recognise your good deeds and so praise God on the day of his coming. (1 Pet 2:12).

This is expanded in the very next verse:

> For the sake of the Lord submit yourselves to every human authority: to the emperor, who is the supreme authority, and to the governors. (1 Pet 2:13)

The early Christians, at least in New Testament times, played safe. They didn't want to exaggerate the threat of persecution, so human expediency forced them to be as loyal to the powers that be as possible. As we shall see when we come to look at the Book of Revelation, that diplomatic loyalty was, for the most part, only a veneer. When the state became undubitably evil, different arguments came to the fore.

These same readers were undergoing a certain amount of persecution, and were being encouraged not to look at their persecutors, but at Christ. (3:15) 'Even if you should suffer for doing what is right, how happy you are!' (3:14) The writer, in the next chapter, goes on to give a very good summary of the early Christian attitude to persecution. For our own purposes, merely note that his emphasis is not on the powers that be, but rather on the eternal context in which both persecuted and persecutor will be judged:

> My dear friends, do not be surprised at the painful test that you are suffering, as though something unusual were happening to you. Rather be glad that you are sharing Christ's sufferings, so that you may be full of joy when His glory is revealed. Happy are you if you are insulted because you are Christ's followers; this means that the glorious Spirit, the Spirit of God, is resting on you. If any of you suffers, it must not be because he is a murderer or a thief or a criminal or meddles in other peoples' affairs.

However, if you suffer because you are a Christian, don't be ashamed of it, but thank God that you bear Christ's name.

The time has come for judgement to begin, and God's own people are the first to be judged. If it starts with us, how will it end with those who do not believe the Good News from God ? As the scripture says. 'It is difficult for good people to be saved; what then will become of godless sinners?' So, then, those who suffer because it is God's will for them, should by their good actions trust themselves completely to their creator, who always keeps His promise. (1 Pet 4:12-19)

These sentiments, in which the persecuted look to the last judgement for their vindication, and not to present day realities, are reinforced by the writer to the Hebrews:

Remember how it was with you in the past. In those days, after God's light had shone on you, you suffered many things, yet were not defeated by the struggle. You were at times publicly insulted and mistreated, and at other times you were ready to join those who were being treated in this way. You shared the suffering of prisoners, and when all your belongings were siezed, you endured your loss gladly, because you knew that you possessed something much better, which would last forever. Do not lose your courage, then, because it brings with it a great reward. (Heb 10:32-34)

Later on the same writer suggests that persecution is a punishment sent by God, in which the persecuting authorities are no more than an agent of God: 'Endure what you suffer, as being a father's punishment; your suffering shows that God is treating you as his sons. Was there ever a son who was not punished by his father?' (Heb 12:7) In no case do either of these writers betray any hint of opposition to the state that is persecuting them: 'For there is no permament city for us here on earth; we are looking for the city which is to come.' (Heb 13:14)

Revelation is very different. Much of the book was written against a background of severe state-inspired persecution, and is couched in an elaborate symbolic code language designed to hide its true meaning in case it should fall into the hands of the wrong people. The power of the Roman empire is described in the blackest of terms. She is pictured as Babylon (17:15), which is the most odious of comparisons to anyone familiar with the Old Testament prophets (cf. Jer 50 and 51) and the deutero-canonical works that were popular at the time (e.g. 2 Baruch 11:1; Sibylline Oracles 5:143; 158; 4 Ezra 2); as a famous prostitute (17:1) who sits on seven hills (17:9), whose seven kings beginning with Nero (54-68 AD) and ending with Domitian (81-96 AD) had all been active persecutors of the church. (17:9) She was adorned with 'names insulting to God' (17:3), which can only be a reference to the divine titles such as 'Lord and God' with which these emperors festooned themselves. The author of Revelation finds all this repellent, since the emperors are usurping the honour due to God and to Christ alone: 'The Lamb will defeat them,' he writes, 'because he is Lord of Lords and King of Kings.' (17:14)

But this violent language does not mean that the writer of Revelation was interested in active civil disobedience, for exactly the same reasons that would have swayed the writers of 1 Peter and Hebrews. It is the Lamb that will defeat the enemy, not any action undertaken by the persecuted. The only civil disobedience that the writers of these books would have countenanced would have been the refusal to recognise the Roman emperor as God. The words of Justin Martyr, who died in about the year 165 AD, ring true to the spirit of the New Testament:

> The Lord said, 'Pay to Caesar what belongs to Caesar; to God, what belongs to God.' Therefore we render worship to God alone, but in all other things gladly obey you, acknowledge you as kings and rulers of earth, and praying that in you the royal power may be found combined with wisdom and prudence.' (*Apologia* 1: xvii)

Polycarp, when faced with interrogation by the Governor of Smyrna at his 'trial', immediately prior to his execution, is recorded to have said:

> … we have been taught to pay all proper respect to powers and authorities of God's appointment, so long as it does not compromise us. (Martyrdom of Polycarp, x.)

Revelation does go further than any other book in the New Testament in denouncing the Roman authorities. We have already seen the less than complimentary descriptions meted out in chapter 17; but the author does not limit his derogatory comments to that chapter. In chapter 13 he pictures the Roman state as being of satanic origin, allowed by God (13:7), but certainly not instituted by him or condoned by him. Yet the denunciation is a strictly internal matter, to be read by other Christians only. As for their public face, these same Christians insisted that they were loyal citizens of the empire in everything save their refusal to bow to the 'divinity' of the emperor. The foundations had been laid for civil disobedience, but as yet the only way that the Christian community was prepared to work for structural change in society was through prayer. Given their small numbers and their impotence, that was the only realistic option open to them.

So far our discussion seems to reinforce Hanson's verdict that the 'New Testament is stony ground for those who are seeking a gospel of social revolution or even of social reform.' But that would be a simplistic, almost naïvely fundamentalist view of the evidence. Taken overall, the New Testament lays the foundation from which the Christian community must learn to be critical of its society, and work, at the very least, for reform. Jesus' preaching of the Kingdom, in which the last shall be first, and the first last (Mt 20:16); his deliberate working within the tradition of the Old Testament prophets, with all their emphasis on social criticism and justice (Mt 23:23; Lk 11:42; Mt 11:4-6); his radicalising and redirecting of human relationships (Jn 4:1-42; Mk 7:24-30; Jn 13:1-20; Mt 5:1-48); his breaking down of the distinction between friend and enemy (Mt 5:44) and between neighbour and foreigner (Lk 10:25-37) 'must necessarily lead to a commitment to support the emergence of a new social consciousness and a new relationship among people.' (Gutierrez, *A Theology of Liberation*, p 234) Jesus' ministry, in which the Kingdom of God was made actual in this present age (Lk 11:20), must challenge his followers to bring that Kingdom about, with the help of Christ, in their own day. That is not to say that Christians must work to replace capitalism with socialism, Marxism, liberalism or any other -ism; but it is to say that a radical criticism of injustice and hypocrisy (such as Jesus meted out to the Pharisees), a preferential option for the poor, and a real change in the personal and communal lives of those who belong to the Kingdom, will itself be revolutionary. Such an incarnation of Jesus Christ today will inevitably change the values and processes of our society in Northern Ireland, in Latin America, the European Union, or wherever. Insofar as it

fails to do so, it fails to bring Christ into the current situation. The
Christian statement is revolutionary. It transcends the merely 'spiritual' and 'political' realms, as commonly understood; it transcends
mere party politics and denominational traditions, to act as an *agent
provocateur*, a challenge to all political systems, for all fall short of
the values and intentions of the Kingdom.

Our Lord, as we have seen, never allowed the temptations to
temporal power to overwhelm him. Whereas Muhammad, the
founder of Islam, took up the sword and the reins of government
when faced with a crisis, Jesus refused them, choosing rather to
undermine his opponents by accepting all that they had to throw at
him. The path that Jesus followed is the very antithesis of the road
to power and influence and is, of its very nature, a standing criticism
of and rebuke to all such paths. He is not just saying 'political
power is not for me.' He is not even saying 'political power is not
for my followers.' He is saying something even more devastating:
'political power and political structures, in all their forms, are totally
inadequate vehicles for the expression of the Kingdom of God'.
'What seems to be God's foolishness is wiser than human wisdom,
and what seems to be God's weakness is stronger than human
strength.' (1 Cor 1:25)

Instead of power, Jesus took the road of service. He washed his
disciples' feet and told them 'You call me teacher and Lord, and it is
right that you should do so, because that is what I am. I, your Lord
and teacher, have just washed your feet. You then should wash one
anothers' feet. I have set an example for you, so that you will do just
what I have done for you.' (Jn 13:13-15) He sets the example, and
then calls us to follow.

Let me explain.

The contrast between the path chosen by Jesus, and the path that
was so often being pressed upon him by his associates and supporters is obvious, and has been spelled out in some detail already. The
road of the incarnation, from beginning to end, was one of compas-
sion (suffering with the people) and not of domination. The cruci-
fixion is a fairly extreme statement of Christ's refusal to take up the
levers of power that were on offer. Paul calls this *kenosis* (*kenosis*:
self-emptying, giving up all that he had, Phil 2:7), and recommends
it as a path for the disciples of Christ:

The attitude you should have is the one that Christ Jesus had: he

always had the nature of God, but he did not think that by force
he should try to become equal with God. Instead, of his own free
will he gave up all that he had, and took the nature of a servant.
He became like man, and appeared in human likeness. He was
humble, and walked the path of obedience all the way to death,
his death on the cross. (Phil 2:58)

If our call as Christians is to be one with Christ, and to follow his
example, then we must take this very seriously. It would seem to
suggest that party politics and high-profile media-oriented leadership are ruled out. If our desire is to 'know Christ and to experience
the power of his resurrection, to share in his sufferings, and become
like him in his death' (Phil 3:10), if we are to effectively 'carry in our
mortal bodies the death of Jesus, so that his life may also be seen in
our bodies' (2 Cor 4:10), then it follows that conformity to his way
precludes the pursuit of political power, from whatever motives.
Our Lord treated it as a satanic temptation: so should we.

Yet it is not true to say that Jesus rejected power in all its forms:
rather, he only rejected power as understood in terms of manipula-
tive domination. The Greek word *exousia* appears forty-two times in
the gospels, nearly always in reference to Jesus, in such phrases as
'He taught with authority' (Mt 7:29; Mk 1:22), 'When the people
saw it they were afraid, and praised God for giving such authority
to men' (Mt 9:8), 'For you gave me authority over all mankind' (Jn
17:2). This is precisely the same word that is used for the authority
wielded by the civil authorities (Lk 12:11), by Pilate (Jn 19:10), the
Roman army (Mt 8:9; Lk 7:8), the chief priests (Acts 9:14), and that
Paul himself uses in the famous passage from Romans 13. Jesus
does have power and authority: but he re-interprets them completely, just as he re-interpreted the whole concept of 'Messiah'. His
authority was constructive, positive, and non-domineering because
he recognised that it was not his own. (Jn 5:30) He saw himself as
coming 'with (his) Father's authority' (Jn 5:43), which probably
explains why it was, and is, so hard for people to come to terms
with. Nothing like it had ever been witnessed before.

Jesus emptied himself of all that we conventionally regard as the
trappings and reality of power. He came alongside the people, and
ministered to them where they were. Right from the beginning he
showed his preference for the marginalised and rejected. His birth
was probably only witnessed by his parents and a few dumb ani-

mals; his first epiphany to the outside world was to a group of awestruck, illiterate and despised shepherds (Lk 2:8-20); he spent his childhood and youth in half-pagan Galilee (Galilee of the gentiles – Is 9:1), far away from the centres of political and religious power, far away from both Torah and Temple; most of his ministry was spent in the countryside, amongst country people, to whom he preached in rural language, with rural illustrations and rural emphases. He spent a great deal of his time with children (e.g. Mk 10:13-16; Lk 9:46-48), with 'publicans and sinners' (e.g. Mt 9:10-13; Lk 7:34), and Samaritans (e.g. Jn 4; Lk 17); and was completely identified with the criminal classes in his death. (Lk 22:37) Conventional wisdom, surely, would suggest a directive approach to these people, using his authority to coerce them into new ways. Instead, Jesus exercises his power and authority in being alongside them, in never once seeking to dominate them, their lives, or their thought. He sought response, and frequently he got response. His effectiveness lay in his consistent rejection of dominant power. He followed his own advice: 'The greatest one among you must be your servant.' (Mt 23:11; cf. Mk 9:35; 10:43-44; Lk 22:26) Jesus was the supreme non-conformist, not just for the sake of attracting attention to himself, but in order to underline the fact that the values of the Kingdom were not those of his day, and not those of our day either. Paul repeats the message: 'Do not conform yourselves to the standards of the world...' (Rom 12:2) In that lies a very severe criticism of the norms of any society.

Jesus was not primarily concerned with charity, in the sense of giving to the poor and needy, mitigating the worst effects of society's failures. There are recorded instances of this (e.g. Jn 13:29), yet they are peripheral to his ministry. In sharing the lot of the poor, in having nowhere to lay his head, he gave of himself. By being alongside them, largely ignoring the structures of domination, production, control and exchange, he showed the essential compassionate solidarity of God. Christ was himself God's gift to all men, particularly the marginalised.

This point is central to much of the gospel material, but is perhaps most importantly so in the Beatitudes of Matthew 5:1-12, and in the parable of the sheep and the goats (Mt 25:31-46). In the Beatitudes, Our Lord gives a list of eight different kinds of people who are to be considered 'happy' (blessed). They are: those who know that they are spiritually poor; those who mourn; the humble; those whose greatest desire is to do what God requires; the merciful; the pure in heart; the peacemakers and the persecuted. Hardly a list with which the advertising industry or Hollywood would concur! These are blessed because they have no claim on God or man. They are blessed because Christ is beside them, in solidarity with their condition.

In Matthew 25 we move on in time to the last judgement, in which the righteous are thoroughly surprised that they should be regarded as righteous at all. Having been congratulated by the King on all the good things that they have done, they respond in utter amazement by saying, 'When, Lord, did we ever see you thirsty and give you a drink? When did we ever see you a stranger and welcome you into our homes, or naked and clothe you? When did we ever see you sick or in prison and visit you?' In response to this very understandable question, the King replies 'I tell you, whenever you did this for the least important of these brothers of mine, you did it for me.' (Mt 25:37-40) Without realising it, they had met and ministered to Christ himself as they worked among the marginalised.

We have established that Jesus did not use the levers of temporal power to achieve his goals; that he chose rather to empty himself of anything that conventional wisdom regards as power or influence, choosing rather to live in non-dominating solidarity with the marginalised and discarded of his day. His plan of action was, understandably, not understood. It was interpreted as highly political. Its very radicalness, in deed and word, was an affront to those in power, both secular and religious. They were forced either to ignore him, or to accept the implications of what he was doing and saying, or to reject him as dangerous. Most took the latter path. They tried him, condemned him, and crucified him. Christ's way, despite its rejection of power, authority, influence and political mechanism, as commonly understood, is inevitably interpreted in these very terms by those it threatens. Therein lies its effectiveness.

Both Mahatma Ghandi and Martin Luther King, two gurus of the twentieth-century peace movements, learned a great deal from Jesus, and were open about the fact. But I suspect that they went beyond what Christ would have done, at least in terms of active opposition to the powers that they were opposing. They renounced physical violence. So did Jesus (with one exception – Jn 2:13-22). They rejected the taking of human life as a means of procuring justice. So did Jesus. But they went on to use these ideals as a power-base from which to stir the people into action. Jesus did not. He rejected that path, and was in turn rejected by the people because of it.

This of course begs a huge question: how much are we called to a literal imitation of Christ in today's world? Our situation is very different from his. He was an initiator; we are inheritors. He was God incarnate: we are not. The arguments are many, and they are strong. But every time I am tempted to accept them, I am reminded of the parables of the Kingdom, in which Jesus likens the Kingdom to leaven (Mt 13:33), to a seed (Mt 13:31-32), to salt (Mt 5:13), and to a candle (Mt 5:14-16). Leaven and salt are useless unless they are mixed with food; a seed is useless unless it falls into the ground and disappears; a candle stays put and gives out its light just by being. The Christian, the ambassador of the Kingdom (Eph 6:20), is in a similar position. He is there to be in solidarity with all men, especially the marginalised, to support, encourage, challenge, and conscientise them, but ultimately so that they can become masters of their own destiny. Ghandi and King manipulated the people (from the best of motives, and towards the best of goals). Christ did not and, as a result, his impact was far more permanent in the long term. People became aware of his significance because he refused to manipulate them in any way. Christ made people aware of themselves and their situation: so today the Christian seeks to do the same. The Kingdom grows out of people's response to that. On the face of it, Christ's following the road to Golgotha was not just suicide, it was political madness. It was a weird and nonsensical way to offer men freedom. And so today our bias should be in favour of following that road, even if it only leads to 'failure'.

By his choice of incarnation, and by his management of the choices offered him during that incarnation, Jesus criticised the very fabric of society (all societies). He challenged men and women to re-examine their human relationships, and to re-work them on the model of service and identification with the marginalised. These challenges remain with us and must cause us to ask questions about the world we live in, and to examine the extent to which it measures up to the ideal of the Kingdom projected by Our Lord.

Does our society offer justice for all? The Old Testament is full of references to justice (28 of them) and judgement (316 of them). The prophets, as we saw in chapter 1, are full of denunciations of injustice, and of appeals to the people and their leaders to be true to their covenant obligations to provide justice. The word *judgement* has unfortunate connotations today: originally it meant judgement in favour of the righteous, the poor and oppressed, the widow and the fatherless. Interpreted in this way, it is a central theme of the Old Testament, and one which is taken up in the New. By working within the prophetic tradition, Jesus takes it up, both implicitly and explicity, and in his own unique way he deepens its implications. He emptied himself, and took sides with the poor, the oppressed, and even the unrighteous. He came to proclaim 'the acceptable year of the Lord.' (Lk 4:20, in the authorised *King James Version*) This is a quotation from Isaiah 61:2, and refers to the Jubilee in which 'all property that has been sold shall be restored to the original owner or his descendents, and anyone who has been sold as a slave shall return to his family.' (Lev 25:10) He was challenging his contemporaries with the literal meaning of the Law and the Prophets. Is there justice for all? Is there a fair distribution of wealth?

Today we must ask the same questions, and where the answer to those questions is 'No', we have a duty to work for change in the way that Jesus did or, and this is not necessarily the same, in the way in which we believe that he would work today, were he in our position. Despite all I have said so far, we cannot just sit back and let the Kingdom float down on the clouds of heaven. Just as in Mt 25 the righteous were deemed righteous because they cared for the marginalised, so we too should work among them. We will be judged on the basis of what we have done, not merely on what we have believed (cf. Ps 62:12; Mt 16:27; Rom 2:13,16; 1 Cor 3:8; Jas 2:24; Rev 20:12):

> Not everyone who calls me 'Lord, Lord' will enter the Kingdom of heaven, but only those who do what my Father in heaven wants them to do. When the judgement day comes, many will say to me, 'Lord, Lord! In your name we spoke God's message, by your name we drove out many demons and performed many miracles!' Then I will say to them, 'I never knew you. Get away from me, you wicked people!' (Mt 7:21-23)

It seems that to work for the Kingdom is not necessarily the same as being overtly religious (cf. Is 1). God is not beyond using heathens to fulfil his purpose (cf. Is 45:1).

We ask the questions that Jesus asked, and we try to work for the values that he espoused. Throughout the gospels these values are expressed in very concrete terms. The doers of 'religious' works get short shrift from Our Lord: the blessed of the Beatitudes and Matthew 25 are not those who do the religious thing. This should make the professionally religious like myself very uncomfortable.

Jesus let go of his divine prerogatives. On occasions he specifically asked inquirers to do the same with their human prerogatives. The rich young man who asked him what he needed to do to receive eternal life was told to sell all that he had, and to give the proceeds to the poor. (Mk 10:21) The man who wanted to go and bury his father before acting on his response to Jesus' call was told, somewhat brusquely, 'Let the dead bury their own dead. You go and proclaim the Kingdom of God.' (Lk 9:60) To another he said 'Anyone who starts to plough and then keeps looking back is of no use to the Kingdom of God.' (Lk 9:62) The demands of the Kingdom are urgent. They require a total dedication, a willingness to let go of wealth, privilege, social and family responsibilities. Jesus let go of such things, and set the world ablaze.

The same is true of the church. The small mission halls that bespeckle the Shankill Road in Belfast have little or no social respectability, yet they change people. The Ethiopian Church after the revolution of 1974 changed from being a largely moribund church in an ailing empire, to being a suspect counter-revolutionary agency. It was persecuted, many of its leaders were executed, it dwindled in numbers and it began to pray. Now, twenty years later, the Ethiopian Churches are fuller than they have ever been before, and the Marxist régime of Mengistu Hailemariam is no more. The churches of Eastern Europe (when it still called itself a socialist society), were filled to overflowing and played a vital rôle in the eventual and peaceful collapse of the system. Similarly, the newly-opened cathedrals of Communist China are bursting at the seams. The church's impact on the lives of individuals and communities is in almost inverse proportion to its identification with the status quo. Part of the attraction of these churches is the fact that, by their very existence, they challenge the prevailing mores of society. Most western churches have sadly lost that witness.

Throughout history, the church has opted all too often for the comfort of the status quo, despite the heartening (if limited) examples of the last paragraph. It has quoted Romans 13 and closed the book, assuming that the case has thereby been adequately stated. But this is a sad travesty of the spirit of Christ and the gospel. The church should always move with eyes and ears and heart open to the sores of society, to those areas in which society falls short of the values of the Kingdom of God. The church should have a preferential option for the poor, should identify with the poor and assist them in their self-realisation.

The church is not primarily concerned with political action, save insofar as compassionate solidarity will always be interpreted as political. Yet, this does not mean that Christians (who are the church) can sit back and do nothing in situations of injustice and oppression. They must, like Christ, go in and get their hands dirty in compassionate solidarity. They cannot argue that, since the Kingdom is a gift that depends on grace, they are excused from doing anything about it. Jesus' whole life was one of active involvement, if of a rather special kind. While the Rabbis of his day, like Hillel, said 'Never do to anyone else anything that you would not want someone to do to you.' (cf. Tob 4:15), Jesus said 'Do for others just what you want them to do for you.' (Lk 6:31) His was an ethic, not just of avoiding evil, but of positively going out to do the good. So too for us today.

To summarise, the New Testament, like the Old Testament, persistently challenges the assumptions of those who wield power. Jesus' message is an abrasive challenge to those with wealth and authority but it is a constructive criticism. Jesus, unlike parts of the Old Testament, never supported violent revolution. Following his example, the rest of the New Testament writers are content to fight shy of anything that might be so construed. There is no New Testament support for those who would like to upset the political equation by using force.

Christ's life and witness involved solidarity with the marginalised. It involved a radical plea that the Old Testament laws concerning justice and equality be taken seriously. As such he was a living criticism of the society in which he lived. Yet at the same time he did not choose to live out this criticism by taking up the political cudgels, or by leading campaigns. He chose rather to empty himself, to renounce all semblance of power, and to identify with those at the bottom of the pile and share their lot. He calls us to do the same. Quite how is the subject of the rest of this book.

CHAPTER 3

Peace

Before we move to a more general application of the biblical insights we have examined, we need to take a look at one more concept – peace – which is interpreted in some quarters in a highly apolitical and subjective sense. A good example of this is Dr Dickenson, then Moderator of the Presbyterian Church in Ireland, who in his Christmas and New Year message 1985/1986, entitled 'Sweet Peace – the Gift of God's Love' says:

> Peace can only come into the world in God's way and in God's time. God's peace is not a ceasefire between warring rivals. God's peace is not a negotiated settlement between disputing parties. God's peace is not a political solution to racial or religious animosities ...'

Is that really what the Bible says? The Old Testament word usually rendered 'peace' in our English versions is *shalom*. It is generally recognised that this is an inadequate translation, a fact that is borne out by the variety of other words that are used to translate it throughout scripture – such as *favour* (Song of Sol. 8:10 *GNB*), *good health* (Gen 43:28 *AV*), *prosperity* (Jer 33:9 in both versions), *safe* (Job 15:21 *GNB*), *success* (Ps 35:27 *GNB*), *rest* (Ps 38:3 *AV*), *welfare* (Jer 29:7 *RSV*) etc. We can get a fuller idea of what this word means if we look at the contexts in which it appears.

A biblical perspective
In Isaiah 9:2-7, a passage that Christians have always regarded as referring to Our Lord, we hear these words:
A child is born to us! A son is given to us!
And he will be our ruler.
He will be called 'Wonderful Counsellor',
'Mighty God', 'Eternal Father',
'Prince of Peace'.

As Prince of Peace, what does his work involve? It involves the giving of joy (v. 3), and the breaking of the yoke of oppression (v. 4). He will base his power on right and justice (v. 7). This theme, in which justice and peace are seen as handmaids, is echoed frequently in other parts of the Old Testament (e.g. Is 32:15-20; Ps 72: 1-4; Zech 8:16-17). In these passages, and in many others, peace is seen as more than a mere absence of war: it is a total state of society in which wickedness has been routed, and justice and righteousness are in control. It is an ideal that includes not only the absence of war (Lev 26:6; Mic 5:5), but also prosperity and success (Ps 35:27; 37:11; 122:6-7; 128: 5-6).

So peace, as understood by the Old Testament writers, is more than the absence of war. It includes concepts such as wholeness, justice, joy, the ending of oppression, righteousness, prosperity, truth, honesty, success, security, long life, blessing, the absence of fear. That being the case, it must *include* 'ceasefires between warring rivals ... negotiated solutions to racial or religious animosities.' The Old Testament concept of peace is not exhausted by these, but it most certainly includes them.

Dr Dickenson, and those who follow his line of argument, are right in saying that God's peace is his gift to us, but wrong in implying that, because it comes from God, we should not seek to negotiate and work and struggle for the conditions in which it is most likely to thrive. Food also comes from God, but we have to work for it!

Peace comes from God, yet for it to appear on earth at all, it has to be our human achievement – at least, this side of the apocalypse! (Is 26:12) Jeremiah, when writing to the exiles in Babylonia, tells them to 'work for the good (*shalom*) of the cities where I have made you go as prisoners. Pray to me on their behalf, because if they are prosperous (*shalom*), you will be prosperous (*shalom*) too.' (Jer 29:7) There it is: work for *shalom*. We may not be the initiators, but our effort and cooperation are vital to the purposes of God.

Jesus, well versed in the scriptures, was fully aware of all this. When he came as Prince of Peace, bringing with him the Kingdom of God, he was not just coming as the purveyor of a personal salvation. He brought his original and highly critical mind to bear on the whole complexity of human relationships. In his preaching of peace (Jn 14:27) he was re-echoing and deepening all that had gone before him in the Old Testament. He did not reinterpret peace to the same

extent as he reinterpreted concepts such as Messiah and power, yet
he does give it his own special stamp.

This limited reinterpretation is most apparent in such passages
as:

> Do not think that I have come to bring peace to the world. No, I
> did not come to bring peace, but a sword. I came to set sons
> against their fathers, daughters against their mothers ... (Mt
> 10:34-35; cf. Lk 12: 49-53)

Our Lord was aware that his message can be very disruptive, and in
its radicality can cause misunderstanding and dissension. The
urgency of the gospel being so great, it was inevitable that it would
demand sacrifices and a willingness to let go, leave behind, and
sometimes even offend loved ones. But this division is a result only
of the misunderstandings engendered by the gospel, and the negative reactions it can sometimes evoke. It is not part of the gospel
message itself.

The peace that Christ offers can only come as a result of a commitment to the person of Christ. (Lk 7:50; 8:48; 19:42-44) It grows
out of the new relationship with God that is the result of Christ's
work (e.g. Rom 5:1; Col 1:20). It is a subjective thing, at least in part
– but our Lord would have been horrified to see that subjective sal-
vation/healing/peace divorced from its Old Testament roots of
justice/righteousness/prosperity. And what is more, it is something to be worked for:

> What good is there in your saying to them 'God bless you!' (liter-
> ally, 'Go in peace'), 'Keep warm and eat well' – if you don't give
> them the necessities of life? (Jas 2:16)

What is the use of wishing someone peace (as every Arabic,
Hebrew, Somali and Swahili speaker does almost every day) if we
do not strive to ensure that the conditions are favourable for the fulness of that peace to thrive?

In Ephesians 2:14-15, Paul talks about the peace that Christ has
brought between Jew and Gentile by the 'breaking down of the wall
that separated them.' This passage has special relevance to us in
Northern Ireland, where the obvious and deep divisions between
Christians are a direct denial of the peace of Christian fellowship,
and where five-metre-high walls have been built to keep our communities apart. Wherever men and women are concerned with pro-

claiming the Kingdom of God, they must also be concerned with the breaking down of barriers. In Paul's argument, that breaking down of the barriers *preceded* the creation of the New Nation within the Kingdom. So long as there are barriers between people there is only a limited evangelism, and only a sorry parody of the Kingdom. Christ's peace demands a serious attempt at reconciliation between warring rivals and disputing parties, if it is ever to progress from words to reality. Christ has brought us peace – but *we* have to bring it. We are the agents of his peace just as much (or as little) as we are agents of his salvation.

So the New Testament concept of peace fills out that of the Old Testament. It includes justice, righteousness, absence of war, reconciliation. It demands that the Christian 'turn away from evil and do good; he must strive for peace with all his heart.' (1 Pet 3:11) It demands a constant struggle against individual and public alienation, private and structural sin. Perhaps, on the basis of the New Testament, we should rephrase Dickenson: God's peace demands that we work for negotiated settlements between disputing parties; God's peace is incomplete without a political solution to racial or religious animosities.

The biblical call for peace is a vital one. So, as we saw in the first two chapters, is the call for justice. Both are intimately related to the concept of idolatry, for to commit injustice, and to fail to work constructively for peace, is to ignore God and his call to selflessness. To commit injustice, or even to permit it, is to ignore the image of God in those who are being subjugated (Gen 1:26); it is to worship the false God of our own selfish interest. By doing that we bring judgement upon ourselves.

It must be fully apparent by now that the whole concept of 'Kingdom of God' has two dimensions that must not be divorced. The first is the socio-political dimension that we have argued somewhat laboriously contra Dickenson, and the second is the personal, internalised dimension, well summed up in the phrase 'The Kingdom of God is within you'. (Lk 17:21) Our Lord came to save the whole person, and just as people live an incomplete humanity so long as they are denied justice, the opportunity of satisfying employment, or decent housing etc., so too they cannot live a complete humanity if the inner liberation of Christ is rejected or ignored.

Bearing this in mind, I propose to ask, in very general terms, the very same questions thrown up in the last chapter. Does our society today grant justice? Does it offer a fair distribution of wealth?

According to the *Oxford English Dictionary*, justice is the quality of being morally just or righteous, the principle of just dealing. That definition is perhaps not very helpful, almost a tautology. Justice certainly involves righteousness, both in interpersonal relationships and on a wider plane, be it national or international; it certainly includes the idea of fairness – fair wages, fair prices; it excludes bribery, exploitation, imprisonment without trial, rigged courts, rigged elections, gerrymandered constituencies; it excludes any imbalance of opportunity based on race, colour or religious affiliation. That is, and must be, a minimum definition of justice. How far does our society today measure up?

It is almost enough just to ask the question. Anyone could give examples of short-fall under each heading: unfair wages in the clothing industry, both here and in Taiwan or Bangladesh; outrageously see-saw prices for the commodities produced by the less developed countries; kickbacks and overblown expense accounts in the city; exploitation of tea-estate workers in Sri Lanka or salt-mine slaves in Mali; imprisonment without trial in half the countries of the world; rigged courts in Iran; rigged elections in Guyana or the Philippines; gerrymandered constituencies in most 'democracies', including our own; racial discrimination in England; religious discrimination in Northern Ireland. The list could grow to fill the remaining pages of the book.

Let's attempt to be more specific. Unemployment, despite state benefits, is not just a misfortune. It is a social evil that grows out of fundamental inequality of opportunity. This is not to point the finger and say (as is fashionable) 'It's all the government's fault'; it is not as simple as that. Neither can we blame it all on capitalism, for the socialist states, where they claimed to have full employment, were only papering over the cracks by giving people non-jobs such as sitting at the top of escalators in Seremetyevo airport in Moscow. All systems try to keep their failures quiet by paying them hush money, either in the form of benefits or wages for doing unnecessary and unsatisfying jobs. There is no -ism or system that has yet offered a reasonable equality of opportunity, and I am not sure that there ever can be. There is no ordering of human society that has yet been even remotely just, and again I am not sure that there ever can be. But that does not mean that Christians can just opt out of any attempt to achieve it, or ameliorate the worst effects of its failures.

Perfection is impossible this side of the *parousia*. But improvement is possible. There must be a better, fairer way of setting wages and wage differentials, of commodity trading, of regulating the financial markets. I am not an economist, so I will not attempt to propose one. But I am sure that there are Christian economists, commodity traders and financiers who could do so. There must be a better way of maintaining the balance of east/west relations than the lunatic concept of Mutual Assured Destruction, and thank heaven that many, with a better grasp of the issues than I, are working to find it.

These are fields for experts, in which the layman feels powerless (which is surely an alienating injustice in itself). But there are areas closer to home in which each and every person, Christian or otherwise, can and should work for improvement. The non-Christian, or someone motivated by other than religious factors, can do this from sheer altruism, genuinely wanting to work for justice and the improvement of whatever situation he or she is tackling – housing, welfare of prisoners' dependents, widows, pensioners, playgroups, drug addicts etc; the Christian works from these motives too, yet with the added dimension that he or she knows that he or she is working towards a divine ideal of which he or she is as yet only simply aware. The Kingdom of God is at hand.

The Christian, however, does not merely work for an improved system, or the improved material circumstances of the underprivileged. The Christian realises that individuals have to be changed, to be made aware of their position, both moral and social. Whatever jargon phrases are used – born again, saved, atoned for, put right with God, forgiven, justified, etc. – the Christian is working on two fronts: the personal (spiritual) in which men and women are confronted with the deepest realities about themselves and their possibilities; and the wider question of society and how it is to be improved. The latter without the former is mere activism, only tinkering with superficialities; the former without the latter is nothing more than pietism, sadly unrelated to the realities of the world, or of faith.

With these considerations in mind, it is hardly surprising to see that Christians have been in the forefront of struggles for justice all over the world: Chile, Argentina, Nicaragua, Haiti, Uganda, Burma, Poland, the Soviet Union, the Philippines, South Africa, to name but a few. It is rather sad to see how conspicuously absent from such struggles (and I do not mean the armed struggle) individual Christians and churches have been in Northern Ireland. Northern Irish Christianity, particularly in its Protestant and Anglican forms, has here fallen woefully short of, if it has not totally ignored, the challenge of the gospel. It has avoided the prophetic call to justice, and Christ's amplification of that message, to concentrate instead on pietistic individualism, with a socio-political bolt-hole in Romans 13. This needs to be analysed, and that is the task of the next few chapters.

CHAPTER 4

Politics

'As a Unionist I seek nothing for myself which I will not gladly share with all my fellow citizens. But I am equally adamant that I shall have none with privilege over me.'
— Frank Millar, Chief executive of the Ulster Unionist Party, *Belfast Telegraph*, 15 January, 1986.

Frank Millar's use of the word 'privilege' is revealing. For it is the holding of perceived privilege that is at the root of so much of the Northern Ireland problem. Today, many of us in the unionist tradition feel that we have lost the advantage, that the 'other side' are now in the ascendant. This perception, whether justified or not, is none the less real – as real as the nationalist perception of unionist privilege has been for the past seventy years. Today many of us unionists feel that we have been betrayed, or are about to be betrayed, by the very power to which we held ourselves loyal, and we are not sure which way to turn.

In the past the boot was on the other foot. We in the Protestant community felt safely in the ascendant, and our politicians successfully garnered votes by beating the Orange drum. Very successfully they persuaded the working classes of Protestant Ulster that their interests lay together with those of the business and landowning ascendancy. Today's Protestant politicians are no longer from the land-owning ascendancy, and they play different cards. But they are still the cards of a community that is afraid to open itself up to the influence or the ideas of the 'other side'. Behind all these lie the same assumptions: your interests (working class interests) are best served by maintaining the tribal block. Not far beneath the surface lurks the fear that, should tribal solidarity falter, the so-called Protestant inheritance will be swamped by the yellow peril of Home rule/Rome rule.

The assumptions, so convenient both to us and to our politicians, and the old ascendancy (of which I am a son), are false. The Protestant working class of Belfast and Londonderry were not significantly better off than the Catholic working class (and in the field of education, are now significantly worse off in many areas). Both worked long hours for low pay in the mills; both lived in gerry-built little kitchen houses. The Protestant, on the whole, did have a better share of the skilled employment in places like the shipyard and Mackies – but he was still underpaid by international standards, and his work served his employers well. The skilled Protestant worker did not stand to lose either job or opportunity should the Protestant/unionist political ascendancy collapse, for his job depended as much on social convention within the two communities, and on sectarian employment practices, as on the particular policies of the Stormont government. That much is borne out by the continuing need for a Fair Employment Agency (FEA) despite the existence of a government supposedly committed to non-sectarian policies and non-discrimination. The Protestant working class of Northern Ireland, on whose votes the unionist establishment depended, and upon whose labour they grew rich, has been fooled ever since partition. From all points of view, there was a closer identity of interest with the Catholic working class. However, the deeply and honestly held tribal perspective dominant in our island has made sure that that identity of interest was never allowed to mature. The whole community has been poorer as a result.

There have been signs recently that this simplistic equation is beginning to falter. The Alliance Party, often described as 'Unionist with a small "u"', has, since its foundation in the 1970s, prided itself on its non-sectarian nature, and on its willingness to seek new avenues towards a settlement. But it remains small. The old Labour Party has always been with us, but has had a hard time in making its non-sectarian voice heard over the past twenty-five years. But, when not confronted by a television camera or a journalist, many people are beginning to formulate thoughts that would seem to be anathema to the ever-so-public unionist mainstream. The 'new' working class unionist parties (the Ulster Democratic Party and the Progressive Unionist Party) have been saying some remarkably positive and non-sectarian things since they helped to broker the loyalist ceasefire. They have made apologies and talked of forgiveness. They have shown a willingness to consider a far wider range of constitutional and social possibilities than the traditional unionist parties would countenance. But their general acceptance is not helped by their perceived closeness to the paramilitaries, nor has their electoral mandate been tested (save in Newtownabbey, where the result was arguably influenced by an ill-timed leak of the Anglo-

Irish framework document). It is too early to assess either their impact, or their acceptability.

Having said that, however, it is a sad truth that the politics of the Northern Irish Protestant community as a whole are motivated by this narrow tribally-based self-interest, rather than by a broader feeling for the interests of the whole community. This is as true today as it was at the time of the Solemn League and Covenant (28 September, 1912). But then there was, arguably, a sound economic reason for unionism, in that the prosperity of the north-east corner of this island was inextricably bound up with 'across the water'. But now the only strong economic argument, rarely mentioned for fear of frightening the British tax-payer, is the £2000 million annual subvention that keeps the Northern Ireland economy afloat. The unionist call today is not to the economic argument, but to the gut reactions that rebel at the very mention of Dublin or Rome.

Yet gut reaction cannot just be dismissed. There are very good reasons (as well as very bad ones) why we Ulster Protestants have taken the political stances we have. We are an immigrant community, and immigrants are insecure, despite the centuries. We feel threatened, in some way, by the dominant Gaelic culture that surrounds us and are therefore reluctant to place too much trust in that community – especially in view of the fact that we have given them little cause to trust us over the years. We want to preserve our culture and identity, which is a noble aim. Yet, we have hitched all our colours to one mast – the mast of unionism. That is very dangerous. Surely it would be safer, and wiser, to explore every honourable avenue to settlement, a settlement in which all can feel secure. Our current fixation with British links and borders can actually only harm those things that are good and true in our heritage. We weaken that positive heritage by defending it with nothing other than negatives. Let's therefore explore all options – we may be surprised by the joys that we find.

This narrowness of vision is coupled all too often with an absolute unwillingness even to attempt to understand the nationalist aspiration. I remember talking to one young man in my last parish (on the Shankill) who complained bitterly that no one understood, or wanted to understand, the loyalist position. I asked him whether he had made any attempt to understand the nationalist or republican position – and he replied that he had no intention of ever so doing.

Even today when, as has been mentioned, many in our community are beginning to feel something of the alienation from the institutions of state that has characterised nationalist politics since partition, virtually no unionist politician has publically avowed this parallel or attempted to draw any conclusions from it. The illusion of 'being on top' is still maintained. The preservation of power is seen as the only way of allowing our community to flourish – a very dubious assumption from the New Testament point of view. The present crisis of unionism has done nothing to encourage a deeper understanding of the other community, with their aspirations and their anger. There is an alarming unwillingness even to *seek* to understand. Mutual understanding is perceived as threat.

There has been a similar blindness over the past few years amongst those of us who have been complaining about the re-routing of 'traditional' parades. Ian Paisley refers to the freedom to march wherever he wants as a 'basic liberty', and has been reported as saying that it is a liberty he is prepared to die for (*Belfast Telegraph*, 8/7/86). This is a dishonest argument: I cannot see many Orangemen welcoming a republican Easter parade up the Shankill Road.

The situation has changed since 1969, when (arguably) the July season Orange parades could be regarded as a colourful folk-festival to be enjoyed by all sections of the community. The fact now is (whether we like it or not) that this is no longer the case. Orange marches, especially those through nationalist areas, are regarded as insensitive at best, and downright provocative at worst. Orange marches through nationalist areas today are actions likely to provoke a breach of the peace; they are seen as a statement of tribal triumphalism that should have no place in the life of one who seeks to follow the Christ of the gospels.

At the time of writing, within days of the publication of the British/Irish 'Framework for the Future', it is too early to make any definitive comments, either about the document itself, or about reactions to it. Initial reactions to the (highly selective) leaks of early February were not encouraging – and the signs are that what we heard then will be repeated again. There seemed then to be very little willingness to contemplate any sort of cross-border institutions, let alone ones with accountable executive powers. There was no sign of any understanding that such institutions would do much to satisfy constitutional nationalists, giving them some form of largely symbolic guarantees from Dublin, just as we get our guarantees from London – although in a far weaker form. 'Not an Inch', although not actually stated, was not far from the surface. The proposals were dismissed, even before they were seen in their entirety, as 'betrayal' and 'conditional surrender'. There was, in all the political posturing, little sign of any willingness to compromise for the greater good of the whole community. There was little sign of any acceptance that, if permanent peace is to be obtained, we will all have to swallow bitter pills.

Those early reactions were acutely depressing to those of us who want to see an inclusive way forward. There seemed to be an almost total unwillingness to discuss anything that was not on 'our agenda'; there seemed to be a blindness to the fears and dreams and legitimate concerns of the other community; there seemed to be an inbuilt assumption that we, as the majority community, had the sole right to suggest what might, or might not, be discussed.

However, in the immediate run up to publication, there were signs of a softening, of a realisation that too much was at stake merely to repeat the old slogans and retire into old bunkers, at least from some of our leaders. Negotiation still seemed to be on offer, despite differences over content, mechanisms and time-scales for that negotiating process. This was encouraging, but, especially in the light of immediate post-publication reaction, it does not go far enough. There is a need to open up the agenda to include the legitimate concerns of others – the nationalist and republican communities are not nationalist out of mere bloody-mindedness. There is a need to trust, perhaps cautiously, but nonetheless to trust all parties involved in this debate. There is no threat of being sold down the river. The document is not a one-way street to a United Ireland, (and even if it were, it is a discussion document, and not a new constitution to be foisted upon us). The British Government has said repeatedly that consent and agreement within Northern Ireland are the absolute ground rules; and the Irish Government has reiterated, yet again, its commitment to the majority principal in the six counties, not least in the words of John Bruton who promised in the Dáil on the 21 February that the people of Northern Ireland would have 'sovereignty in their own affairs vested in themselves'.

Now, in the immediate aftermath of publication, the negatives seem once again in the ascendant. They are, admittedly, qualified negatives; alternative proposals have been tabled, and these proposals are not without merit or even generosity. But there also seems to be an amazing facility by our political representatives to read into the text of the document the exact opposite of what is actually there, to ignore assurances, to refuse to recognise gains for their own point of view. They want to find the worst, and are certainly not predisposed to credit any merit to suggestions that do not

come from our own stable. No one else, it seems, has anything constructive to offer.

The whole attitude, to put it politely, is far too grudging – where
is the generosity of spirit that should be the hallmark of the
Christian and Protestant mind? Where is the real willingness to talk
with an open agenda? Where is the willingness to admit that there
is an Irish dimension (an Irish dimension even to our own personal-
ity as Ulster Protestants), – an Irish dimension that needs more than
toothless committees to give it life? Where is the willingness to take
risks, to be bold for the sake of all? Where is the willingness to see
any merit in anything other than our own ideas? I am saddened,
but the immediate reactions to the new Framework Document suggest that there has been very little change in Protestant attitudes, at
least amongst our leaders. Unionism still dominates; Biblical
Christianity is shoved to the sidelines.

The dominant ethos among our political class is very sad, especially from a so-called 'Protestant' people, led by so many clergy-
men. It seems to be a very far cry from the biblical challenge that we
examined in the first part of this book. Is it a Christian merit to cling
to supposed privilege? Is it a Christian merit to refuse to talk with
those enemies that Christ told us to love? Was it a Christian merit to
dismiss, for seventy-five years, the nationalist cries of alienation
and pleas for justice? Is it now a Christian merit to expect others to
hear our cries of 'foul!' when we ignored theirs for so long? Is it a
Christian merit to seek for a return to Stormont-type 'majority rule'
(the *status quo ante*) while angrily denouncing any suggestion of a
united Ireland (which is, after all, only majority rule in a different,
and geographically more logical, context)? Is it a Christian merit to
seek a monopoly of political power when Christ regarded such
power as a satanic delusion?

These are questions that must be faced not just by the unionist
establishment, but also by everyone from within the Protestant/
unionist tradition, and especially by those who wear their
Christianity on their sleeves. I will not attempt detailed political or
theological answers: the purpose of this book is more to pose questions in the hope that those questions, and the challenges that arise
out of them, will clear the way for radical thinking and constructive
action by our leaders, and especially our unionist leaders.

Is it a Christian merit for us to cling to supposed/perceived
privilege? Or, to put it another way, is there any gospel mandate for
those who would like to preserve the Protestant ascendancy, however defined? I know that very few of us would actually think in

those crude terms, but the broad effect of many of our attitudes is very much the same. In the light of the Old Testament, it is perhaps tempting to say that, just as the prophets looked back to the 'good old days' of the Mosaic and Davidic ideals as their models for the future, so too we can justifiably strive for the restoration of a Stormont-style majority rule. But this is nonsense. There are no parallels whatever between the old Stormont model and that of the biblical covenants. The 1921 settlement is hardly a covenant in the Old Testament sense. These covenants were based firmly on a relationship between God and the people of Israel; they may have included a political expression (the Davidic one most certainly did), but they did not receive their identity from that political expression. The Old Testament covenants were theological, not constitutional. Northern Ireland has never had a man of the stature of David to look back to; our constitutional arrangements have never been even remotely akin to the laws of Moses.

Many of our politicians would deny that they are trying to preserve the Protestant ascendancy. They prefer to use such words as 'Protestant values', 'Protestant heritage', 'majority rule', 'majority rights', 'religious freedom'. But, whatever label they put on their policies, the general drift is the same: majority (Protestant) rule is the only sure way of protecting these things, and others that are rightly held dear. There may be talk of power-sharing, and indeed proposals have been put forward to this effect – but it is reluctant power-sharing, which makes it very clear who 'the majority' are. But surely these things, if they have any real value, will prove resilient enough to flourish under a more pluralist, powersharing, or even (dare I say it?) united Ireland régime. We are right to wish to preserve that which is true, noble, right, pure, lovely and honourable (cf. Phil 4:8) within our own culture – that is a noble aim. But to be fixed on only one method of achieving that aim is, at the very least, extraordinarily bad policy. But it is more than just bad policy – it is based on something very deep within our historically conditioned psyche: and that something is a deep seated distrust of the 'other side'. The old cry is not far beneath the surface: 'A Protestant Parliament for a Protestant people.' What a tragedy. Our culture, our faith, our heritage, our way of living, is a vibrant thing, vibrant enough to survive any change of system. It is more at risk of atrophy if it is allowed to turn in on itself and become insecure and defensive. It can only thrive if it goes out to meet others on equal terms, and in the give-and-take of normal life grows and changes and develops as every culture must. We are not a museum people.

We must begin to face the real world, otherwise we will terminally damage that which we claim to love and protect.

* * *

Is it a Christian merit to refuse to talk to your enemies? This may seem to be strong language, but I do not feel that it is so far fetched. Political adversaries across the unionist/nationalist divide have not spoken civilly to each other for any significant length of time since the 'troubles' began. The only serious attempt at communication was stymied by the UWC strike of 1974. The history of not talking in Northern Ireland is as long as it is depressing, and it is continuing today. Rare is the unionist, for instance, who will even acknowledge a Sinn Féin councillor. It frequently sinks to a refusal even to hear a positive remark about certain other people – witness the reaction to Peter Brooke's recent (February 1995) remarks about the positive contribution made by Gerry Adams. This is childish, from wherever it comes, and it only fuels the engines of mistrust, and energises the potential of violence. Ulster will be betrayed, not by those who talk, but by those who refuse to talk.

As we have seen, Jesus did talk to his enemies, although not always very politely. He sat down and had meals with their representatives. (Lk 7:36-50) What is more, he commanded us to love them and pray for them. (Mt 5:44) The call is to perfection (Mt 5:48), and despite all the attractive logical arguments and political expedients that would pull us in the other direction, we listen to them only at the risk of ignoring Our Lord. You cannot love someone with whom you refuse to talk; you cannot love someone to whom you refuse to listen; you cannot love someone whom you do not seem even to want to understand, let alone agree with. Love is not a sentimental affair; in cases such as this it means getting to grips with many deep-seated and understandably negative emotions in order to clear the way for communication and, ultimately, understanding. That requires more courage and strength and humility than all the political posturing of the last twenty-five years. It won't be easy, but surely it is better than a return to violence, with all the pain and grief and unemployment that that has brought with it. Dialogue, with all its risks, is the only responsible, the only Christian, way. 'Jaw jaw,' as Churchill said, 'is better than war war.'

* * *

Was it a Christian merit to dismiss for the last sixty-five years the nationalist cries of alienation and pleas for justice? And, is it now a Christian merit to expect others to hear our cries of 'foul!'

when we ignored theirs for so long? Is it true to say that, insofar as they were considered at all, the nationalists cries of alienation within the Northern Irish state since 1920 were dismissed as wilful delusions by unionist politicians and the bulk of the unionist population? Even as late as 1985, when the word appeared for the first time in the public consciousness, unionists were indignant that Bishop Cahal Daly (then Roman Catholic Bishop of Down and Connor) should so much as suggest that there was some reality behind the nationalist claims of alienation. In a sense, it is irrelevant whether that sense of alienation was justified or not: the fact that it was felt, and keenly felt, by so many people should have caused us to try and get to the root causes of it. When, under Terence O'Neill, we tried for a time to do just that, it was far too late. And since the collapse of the power-sharing executive in 1974, we have refused to try anything at all. Ulster Protestants have been saying 'No' for far too long, and are still all too frequently denying that there was anything wrong with the old Stormont régime.

The same is true today, although it is now our own Protestant/ unionist alienation that is the most obvious problem. Interestingly enough, although we ourselves as a people have yet to admit to the reality of the perception of alienation that exists or existed in the nationalist community, the same nationalist community is showing signs of accepting the reality of the unionist fears. This is not to say that they agree with those fears (any more than they would expect us to agree with theirs) but at least there are signs of listening. Since the Hillsborough Agreement and the more recent Downing Street Declaration, many nationalists have show signs of recognising that unionists are feeling something of the same alienation that they once presumed to be exclusively theirs. I only wish that we could be as sensitive.

One example: it rang a bit hollow when unionist politicians started to call for the banning of plastic bullets after the death of the first Protestant to die from injuries caused by one (April, 1986). Before the signing of the Anglo-Irish Agreement, the use of plastic bullets was supported by the overwhelming majority of our political representatives. Some even supported (in their wilder moments) a 'shoot to kill' policy. But when one of our 'own side' died, the tune was very different. Were we so tribally centred that we could not see how our own anger was precisely the same as that felt by the nationalist community since the first baton round was fired back in the 1970s. The fifteen Catholics who had been killed did not seem to count. The nationalist community might as well not exist.

A mutual recognition of the *reality* of fears, without necessarily accepting the *validity* of those fears, is vital for our future in Northern Ireland. I would like to develop this a little by drawing a parallel with my own experience in Papua New Guinea. Although the particular lessons learned were theological (and therefore also pertinent to our next chapter), it does not take much imagination to transfer the lessons or the experience to our Northern Ireland political scene. After all, politics and religion are not totally divorced in our land!

I worked in Papua New Guinea (PNG) for almost three years (1981-1983), during which time I learned a great deal about myself and my own thought processes. It would be hard to find two Anglican Churches more different that the Anglican Church in PNG and the Church of Ireland. In PNG we indulged in all those 'popish' practices so studiously avoided back home: daily 'mass', reservation of the eucharistic elements, eucharistic concelebration, vestments, incense, processions, a developed mariology, complete with thrice daily *angelus*, etc. And I, from the Church of Ireland, with its studiously Protestant heritage, did not find all this easy either to assimilate or accept.

Initially, it was all rather fun – a novelty to be enjoyed, a colour to be appreciated. But that stage did not last long. I soon found that I did not like all these things – most notably the reservation of the eucharistic elements, eucharistic concelebration and the mariology – and that I had worked out detailed theological reasons with which to back up my complaints. Yet, although I found these practices objectionable, I had to concede that others, also Anglican, did not. Many whose faith and integrity I respected found them really helpful. Indeed, these very practices, which acted as a barrier to me, were a pathway which demonstrably brought others closer to Christ. As such, I had to concede, they could not be wrong *per se* (despite my theological rationalisations of Irish Protestant prejudice!) Maybe they were wrong for me. But not wrong universally.

This is an important point – the rationalisation of prejudice. That is the devil who prowls around the courts of theological and political debate, more destructive than any roaring lion. We all do it, especially when we think that we are at our most irrefutable. My time in PNG forced me to examine my theological assumptions very carefully. Did I dislike eucharistic concelebration because I am an individualist? Did I dislike it because we don't do it that way in Ireland? Or did I dislike it because it seemed to obscure the important concept of the priesthood of all believers, and to emphasise the ordained priesthood at the expense of the wider priesthood which we all share? Or was it a combination of all three?

I would not have thought this way before I went to serve in PNG. I would have gone – and did go – into ecumenical debate with an airy-fairy wooliness. I would have tended to ignore any differences on the grounds that we are all grappling with truths that we can never really understand, and that words can never fully express. But I would not have appreciated the other person's point of view – it was there to be side-stepped. Now, after three years of living and working and praying in such a radically different environment, I found myself in a rather different position. I was forced by circumstances to examine precisely how I felt about certain doctrines and practices. I was forced to mould my devotional life around them, and to use them as channels of grace. It was not always easy. I did not always manage to retain a positive attitude – the loneliness and isolation of the missionary life can often find its outlet in negative reactions. Yet, through living within this tradition, through struggling with it and within it, I came to a deeper appreciation of our differences, and of the motivation that lies behind them.

This is essential Anglicanism. Newman saw it as a *via media* – one of which he eventually despaired. Newman failed as an Anglican in that he was not able to appreciate, deep down, the genuine validity of what, superficially, seem to be deeply irreconcilable positions. It is a struggle that does need to be lived – and it was to live it that I went out to PNG in the first place. I do not believe that monolithic Anglican Churches, with monochrome liturgical practices, are being true to their vocation – and the Church of Ireland is in acute danger of being constitutionally monolithic. Now that I have lived the struggle for myself, I have been changed. No longer can I be so certain that my way is the only correct one. I am more open to the possibility that other paths, even paths that I object to for seemingly sound reasons, can be good and helpful and positive for those that follow them. They can indeed be paths along which God can travel to meet us. And that message is relevant well beyond the ecclesiastical sphere.

C.S. Lewis' picture of heaven, in *The Great Divorce*, rings very true. I can picture the saints in heaven, both Protestant and Catholic, laughing at the things they took so seriously on earth. Laughing primarily at themselves and their own kind, not because they were wrong, but because they believed that their way of loving the Saviour was the only valid one. By comparison with the direct

communion that they now enjoy, all our ways on earth must seem
at best indirect and muddled. 'Did I really do that?', 'Did I really
believe that?', they say. But yet they are still with him in heaven,
because they really loved him – whether they went to confession or
not, whether they said the rosary or not, whether they wore vestments or not. I can imagine that we shall all enjoy a good laugh, if
we get to heaven – a laugh at our own expense. The sight I would
most like to see would be Ian Paisley and Cardinal Ó Fiaich having
a good hearty laugh together in Paradise.

And there is another perspective. Different practices, different
theologies, different politics, sit comfortably on different shoulders,
are acceptable to men of different temperaments and cultural backgrounds. Take my boss at the Theological College at which I was
teaching, an ultra-montane Anglo-Catholic. Our differences were
not merely theological, but total. Our whole range of interests, our
whole approach to life, our whole temperaments were different.
Such temperamental differences are bound to react in different
ways with the perfection that is Christ. But the important thing is
that we both reacted, and that we were both changed by him. It
would have been very easy for us to say to each other, Ulster fash-
ion, 'You are not a Christian', and then ignore what our respective
viewpoints had to say to each other. Fortunately we took the harder
way, and sought to understand each other. Now, perhaps no nearer
agreement on some issues, we can at least recognise that we have
both had a meeting with Christ, and that he has revolutionised both
our thinkings. Fortunately again, that has not made us clones.

Bearing this in mind, surely it is true that an essential ingredient
of faith is humility – the humility to admit that 'I might be wrong'.
In faith we march forward, aware at least of the formal possibility
of error (it is that, surely, that distinguishes faith from knowledge) –
that is the Christian way. If we are to tread that path with integrity,
each one of us must try to understand how we, with our genetic
encoding and up-bringing, have reacted to Christ or to the political
reality that surrounds us. Then we must try and do the same with
our neighbour: how has he, with his different genes and different
background, reacted to Christ? We must start with the assumption
that his reaction to the Saviour is every bit as valid as ours. We may
not be able to understand it in all its complexity – but that should
not be a barrier between us. I cannot understand why people like
Wagner – but that is not a barrier to musical appreciation between
us. I still respect their integrity as music-lovers and as people. I hope
that my time out in Papua New Guinea has helped me, in some way,

to understand and appreciate the theological and political equiva-
lents of Wagner-lovers.

This does not, of course, preclude doctrinal or political discussion – far from it. But doctrinal and political it must be, and not dogmatic; not narrowly to convert another Christ-lover to my own
angle of view, but to seek to deepen and broaden both our points of
view, and to be prepared even to correct or modify my own. There
is a real danger that we in Ireland, seldom consorting with
Christians of other denominations, will take as gospel our own
traditions, formulations and prejudices. If we do that we fall, *ex
hypothesi*, into heresy, which is the sin of thinking that words can
ever begin to treat God with the faintest degree of adequacy, and
then mistaking those words for a final statement of the truth itself.
We must recognise, with Ezekiel, that all our verbal stammerings in
these matters are no more than a description of 'the appearance of
the likeness of the glory of God' (Ezek 1:28 *RSV*) – hardly an accurate description of the ineffable. Likewise with almost everything
that divides us.

Now, that short meditation on my experience in Papua New
Guinea may seem to be rather out of place in the present chapter.
But I think not. The lessons that I learned out there (and have since
deepened back here), are of far wider than theological significance.
Right at the heart of our problems is a refusal by an awful lot of people to accept any 'other side' as human in any meaningful sense of
the term. People become labelled entities, stereotypes, unreal.
Christ's salvation gives us back our full humanity (lost in Adam, cf.
Rom 5:12ff), and demands that we treat fellow Christians (even if
we think them misguided) as fully human, fully Christian. The
gospel demands that we follow Christ in the giving of humanity
and dignity to those to whom it has been denied – and that includes
those who *feel*, rightly or wrongly, that their humanity has been
denied. It also includes those to whom we have denied humanity by
consigning them to the stereotyped ranks of 'Catholics', 'fenians',
'republicans', remaining content with the labels without ever taking the trouble to get to the heart of the man or woman to whom we
attached the label.

On a more mundane level, politics in Northern Ireland are not
all that far removed from theology. The fact that 95% of unionists
are Protestant, and 95% of nationalists are Roman Catholic has
encouraged me to attempt to apply the lessons of PNG, at least
intellectually, to the political beliefs of the 'other side'. This, while
not resulting in agreement, has resulted in a recognition that

nationalist grievances do have some validity, and that those who voice them publicly, sometimes violently, do have some integrity. I may disagree very strongly and on principal with the past methods of Sinn Féin, but I am forced to recognise that their *credo* is not wholly inconsistent. This process is far from straight-forward, but it does need to be taken seriously. Otherwise our lack of understanding will grind us all to dust.

* * *

Is it a Christian merit for us to seek a return to a Stormont type 'majority rule' over one with limited 'power-sharing' while angrily denouncing any suggestion of a united Ireland? Surely the basic requirement of a future constitutional arrangement is not its British or Irish dimensions, but that it be just, and fair, and a respecter of human freedom.

That requirement is, of course, a major one. Nationalists, as a whole, do not feel that either Belfast/Stormont or London have fulfilled the necessary minimum conditions. Unionists feel that Dublin can't, especially in view of Articles 2 and 3 of her constitution. Over the past years, each 'side' has given more than ample reason for the other to distrust it. But, yet again, things are not as simple as that. Our loyalty to Britain is not, for the most part, loyalty to Britain at all. It is loyalty, rather, to Britain as a protector against the Home rule/Rome rule threat. That loyalty wavers when Britain seems to be no longer able or willing to fulfil the role demanded of her. We get back to the self-interested, almost xenophobic, insecurity that lies at the heart of so much of our politics. There are many who feel that, if Britain cannot act as guarantor, then stuff Britain: we will guarantee ourselves and do it alone. There are others, still possibly a majority within unionism, who hope somewhat unrealistically that Britain will once again prove to be as loyal to her Northern Irish subjects as her Northern Irish subjects feel themselves to be to her.

This is a crisis for unionism and Ulster Protestantism generally, and one that may yet force us to examine other options, and to begin to talk seriously and constructively with all comers. I hope that this will encourage us to seek new paths, to take risks for the cause of greater peace, justice and prosperity for all; to take risks to ensure that the society that arises out of our current chaos is one that respects and enhances both the identities and the cultures of all – especially at this time of fragile hope. That should be our goal – regardless of the structures finally agreed to ensure it. All options should remain open and negotiable. They should not be valued in themselves (as they now are) but only insofar as they can contribute to the greater peace, justice and prosperity that we all seek.

Unionism can do that. Yet at the moment we are not doing so. Merely to harp on, as we do now, on the impossibility of accepting cross-border committees with executive powers (the minimum requirement of most nationalists) is to condemn us to a permanent stand-off, in which no one ever listens to what the other is saying. What is important, as I cannot tire of saying, is not the border, or the colour of the flag, but rather we ourselves as the people of this island, with our varied identities and loyalties, our culture, our faith. It is these that must be preserved and encouraged, not just the shell in which they currently reside.

* * *

One extremely difficult way out of this impasse, is to take the path of forgiveness:

> If you forgive others the wrongs they have done you, your Father in heaven will also forgive you. But if you do not forgive others, then your Father will not forgive the wrongs you have done (Mt 6:14-15; cf. Mk 11:25-26; Lk 6:37).

> Forgive one another, as God has forgiven you through Christ (Eph 4:32; cf. Col 3:13).

> If they pray to me and repent and turn away from the evil they are doing, then I will hear them in heaven, forgive their sins, and make their land prosperous again (2 Chron 7:14).

When Peter asked Jesus how often he should go on forgiving a brother who persistently sinned against him, Jesus said 'Seventy times seven' (Mt 18:21ff) – in other words, just keep on forgiving, long after it ceases to be reasonable to do so. This statement is followed by the parable of the unforgiving servant, who is severely punished for his hardness of heart in refusing to forgive those who had sinned against him. Our Lord concludes: 'That is how my Father in heaven will treat you unless you forgive your brother from your heart.' (Mt 18:35)

No one need pretend that this quality of forgiveness – or, indeed, any forgiveness – is going to be easy; yet there are many in our community who have managed. The small Pentecostal community in Darkley, who suffered a dreadful massacre in their church back in 1983, are a fine example of a deep and genuine forgiveness. Many others, who have lost loved ones in the troubles, have also managed to forgive. It is rare for me, in the course of my ministry, to visit the home of a murder or a petrol bombing and to find anything other than the desire that 'No one else should have to go through this'. But these have been essentially individual acts, yet to be translated into a communal reality.

Community forgiveness, by all sides, is desperately needed. If we refuse to forgive, or admit our own need of forgiveness, we condemn ourselves to live in a prison of bitterness from which there is no other escape. It may not seem fair, when we have already suffered so much, to have to make the extra effort and shoulder the extra pain that is required to forgive. Yet without it we die. The New Testament word for forgiveness – *aphesis* – carries with it the sense of letting go, like we let go of a helium-filled balloon at the fair ground. Having let go, we can then watch our sins, our hurts, our barriers, float away like a balloon. We need that sort of forgiveness if relationships between the communities on this part of the island of Ireland are ever to be restored.

I would love to see small groups, of no more than six, getting down and listening intently to the 'other side'. Each would speak in turn, uninterrupted; each would listen, restraining their protests. Each would tell how they felt that they had been hurt by the other. And each would say, 'Yes, I accept your hurt. Yes, I need to be forgiven.' In that process both would learn that much of what had hurt them had been exaggerated by legend, and that their stereotypes were largely false. But there is much that genuinely needs to be recognised and accepted and forgiven. This, especially among Christians, needs to be done in the conscious presence of Christ, 'in order to keep Satan from getting the upper hand over us.' (2 Cor 2:11)

For us Protestants, who place so much emphasis on the assurance of being forgiven, the need to reciprocate and extend the forgiveness we have received to others, is central. Paul quotes Psalm 32: 'Happy are those whose wrongs are forgiven, whose sins are pardoned' (Rom 4:7), and in so doing invites parallels with the Beatitudes of Matthew 5. Those whose wrongs are forgiven are united with those who know that they are spiritually poor, with those who mourn, with those who are humble, with those whose greatest desire is to do what God requires. They are at one with the merciful, the pure in heart, the peacemakers, and the persecuted. We discussed the radical implications of this passage back in Chapter 2 – and they are radical implications that are just not seen in our community today. Christ cries out for a society in which the gospel, in all its fulness, is made visible; he pleads that there should, for Christians, be no area of life that does not belong to him, that is not subject to his headship and his Lordship.

In saying this, I am not suggesting that unionism is morally wrong. It is most certainly not. I only seek to be constructively critical of the tradition in which I was born and brought up, and to encourage that tradition to be more open and understanding of others, and hence more attractive and realistic. A brand of politics that has, over the years, succeeded in incurring the approbrium of the entire world (except, perhaps, a few right-wingers in Britain, the USA and South Africa) really needs to start asking itself some pertinent questions: Might my approach be misguided? Might my intransigence not, after all, be a merit? Why does the rest of the world lack sympathy? What unionism needs (and nationalism, liberalism, socialism, conservatism all need as well – but this is a book aimed at my fellow unionists) – what unionism needs is a few more people who take the biblical suggestions and imperatives seriously. For too long our unionism has dominated our Christianity, so that our Protestantism has become the spiritual arm of the unionist parties. For once, let us allow our politics to be dominated by our religion. It is a dangerous suggestion, for it might mean that we will reach some very surprising conclusions. Let us allow the light of Christ to shine on and challenge all our political beliefs. If we fail to do that, we can hardly claim to be Christians at all.

Marx would have loved it; the churches in Northern Ireland today, and indeed throughout the century, are the perfect target for his critique of religion. We Protestants in particular have so emphasised the personal and pietistic side of holiness that we have begun to think of salvation exclusively in those terms. We have forgotten the social dimension of salvation, which played such an important part in the witness of the Old Testament prophets, and which underpinned much of what Our Lord had to say. Peace, justice, relationships and righteousness have been ignored: the churches have become addenda to the unionist parties. The gospel has become the slave of our political aspirations. Such a Christianity hardly deserves the name.

* * *

Is it a Christian merit to seek the monopoly of power or to seek to control the fora in which power is exercised? This is putting the question in a rather black and white form, starker and perhaps bolder than necessary ... But that is, in essence, what we are seeking to do. We seek to protect our values with the false *chimaera* of political power. Can that possibly be in accordance with the faith that we profess?

In the light of what was said in chapter 2, the simple answer is 'No, it is not a Christian merit to seek a monopoly of power'. Indeed, it could be argued on the basis of the evidence presented in that chapter, that Christians should stay right out of the political process, in a manner similar to that adopted by the Mennonites and the Amish. Some may be called to do that, but not all.

Christ, as we have seen, rejected power and authority, insofar as they were understood in terms of domination. He was intensely concerned to be alongside the people, accepting them, affirming them, challenging them. That, surely, is the path for today's Christian politician, instead of the current situation in which they seem rather to echo and affirm the prejudices of one section of the community. They are in the business of massaging their sectarian power base. They refuse to see our community as the whole it could be. They have it in their power to work differently. I wish that they had the courage to do so.

This is obviously a criticism of those who marry a biblical-fundamentalist approach to the Christian gospel with an equally dogmatic and narrowly conceived unionism – honest doubt of any sort is regarded as apostasy. This has had appalling consequences. All brands of unionism have been tainted by it, to such an extent that it is hard for a Roman Catholic to vote unionist, let alone be a member of a unionist party. Protestantism and unionism are not natural bedfellows; in fact, unionism, if it is to be true to itself, is incomplete so long as it remains a merely Protestant phenomenon. The DUP, and to a lesser extent the UUP, have a stranglehold on the province – a domination, a use of implied threat, that is totally alien to the way of Christ and the New Testament. Protestant Christianity in our land has now got an appalling public image as a result. From an evangelical point of view, that is disastrous.

In a way, their politics are those of 'being alongside the people', but only alongside 'our people'. The Syro-Phoenicians (Mk 7:26), the Samaritans (Jn 4) and the Greeks (Jn 12:20) (i.e., the Catholic/nationalist community) whom Christ welcomed and affirmed, are ostracised. There is nothing wrong in unionist politicians' viewing things from a primarily unionist/Protestant perspective (after all, Jesus was sent primarily to the 'lost sheep of the house of Israel' – Mt 15:24); yet their message has for so long been pitched so negatively, and so tribally, that it has in practice excluded all who do not call themselves Protestant. Current unionism does nothing either to accept or affirm the minority community. Indeed, it is our insensitive use of political power that has done more than anything else to alienate them over the years. Our politicians have failed to challenge anyone within our tribal community, not at least in the sense that Jesus did. Rather, they drive everybody into their tribal bunkers and blindly repeat the slogans of yester-year. 'Ulster' has said nothing but 'No' for the last seventy-five years, and the rest of the world (to say nothing of the nationalist community and the British Government) is getting rather bored. True Christian/unionist leadership would seek to challenge the unionist/Protestant people to re-examine their political inheritance, and through critical analysis to come to a new inclusive way forward.

I do not question the right of politicians, or the people, to challenge government policy. This is not just a democratic right: it is also a prophetic duty. Christian leaders have a duty, following the prophets and Christ himself, to engage in constructive opposition to injustice and bad policy. But that injustice must be real injustice. The Hillsborough Agreement, the Downing Street Declaration, or the proposed framework document, hardly fit that bill.

The nub of the unionist argument against the Hillsborough Agreement, or any future settlement that 'dilutes' the sovereignty of the British crown, is that it gives a foreign power a say over our affairs here in Northern Ireland. That is certainly unusual, but is it unjust? Isn't that precisely the way that many nationalists have felt about the British link? *Pace* what was said earlier in this chapter, there is no merit in refusing to admit that Britain is an alien power for nationalists (who have to accept it), while at the same time refusing to accept the tiniest drop of 'foreign' influence in our own affairs. Two perceived wrongs do not make a justice – but we cannot logically oppose the Hillsborough Agreement or the Framework Document while denying a hearing to those who oppose the British link.

Given the root complexity in our situation, a little flexibility is in order, at least in constitutional matters. After all, a constitution is of value only insofar as it guarantees peace and justice and prosperity. As the situation stands here at the moment, none of the available options is guaranteeing anybody any of those things, not because of any inherent defect in the constitutional arrangements themselves, but because of the refusal of one section of the community to recognise the validity of the aspirations or the fears of some other sector of the same community. To withhold that recognition is to withhold justice; which squares the circle: the nationalists perceive injustice from Britain; the unionists perceive injustice from the Republic (and now from Britain as well); the nationalists perceive injustice from the unionists; the unionists perceive injustice from the nationalists. Isn't it about time that we began to listen to each other, and grow out of all this?

The only thing that the current situation threatens is the dream of certain unionists of a return to monopoly power. Since (short of UDI) that is a gonner anyway, why all the fuss? Those who look at Christ, from whatever side, are (or should be) lifted out of their cursed exclusiveness into his all-inclusive love; they are lifted out of the will to dominate and reject, into the will to serve, into his acceptance of all humankind (Acts 3:25; 1 Cor 15:22; 1 Tim 2:6). Much of our politics today has not let itself be touched by Christ. It has, rather, let Christ be walled in by our exclusive ethnic and political loyalties. That is not salvation: that is imprisonment. And I was under the impression that Christ had come to set us free (Jn 8:31-36; Rom 6:22; Gal 5:1). In short, anyone who is 'in Christ' (Rom 12:5; 1 Cor 15:22; 2 Cor 5:17; Gal 3:27) should examine very carefully the morality of any refusal to talk, any refusal to seriously examine all available options. Such attitudes can only be justified if the options proffered (or seen to be proffered) can be proven in the light of the biblical witness to be unjust. As far as I can see, its only 'injustice' lies in the damage it does to our unionist xenophobia and pride.

To conclude, it is very hard to define the *status quo* in Northern Ireland today. The stalemate of direct rule is hardly an adequate arrangement for anybody, and is generally recognised as such. There is such a jumble of aspirations in the Province that a real and lasting peace will require not just leadership, but also a willingness on behalf of the majority of both communities to seek a path of mutual respect. There is also a real need to let go of the slogans of the past in order to seek for a new future. That is a tall order. It is also a positive order. I believe that it grows out of the biblical witness: indeed, it is a biblical imperative. All our *status quos*, real or imagined, fail to live up to the prophetic and Christly ideals; let all our politicians realise that. Then, and only then, can we begin a realistic quest for peace.

Let Paul have the final word: 'If you act like wild animals, hurting and harming each other, then watch out, or you will completely destroy one another.' (Gal 5:15) 'What human nature does is quite plain. It shows itself in immoral, filthy and indecent actions, in worship of idols and witchcraft. People become enemies and they fight; they become jealous, angry and ambitious. They separate into parties and groups ... I warn you now as I have before: those who do these things will not possess the Kingdom of God.' (Gal 5:19-21)

CHAPTER 5

Religion

We must both act as each is fully persuaded in his own mind. Hold fast to that which you believe is most acceptable to God, and I will do the same ... Let all these smaller points stand aside. Let them never come into sight. 'If thine heart is as my heart', if thou lovest God and all mankind, I ask no more: give me thy hand. (John Wesley, sermon on 'The Catholic Spirit', quoted by Kenneth Greet in *The Tablet*, 27 August 1983, p 821)

Everyone must achieve Christian authenticity within the form of his own culture. (E. Schillebeeckx, *God, the future of man*, p 187)

No doubt we could ask Roman Catholics many questions that they could not answer, and they could ask us many questions which we could not answer: we can only each go our own way, holding on to the truth which we know we have. (John Keble to Charlotte Yonge, quoted in R. Chapman, *Faith in Revolt*, p 71)

We have established, I think, that no Christian who takes the biblical witness seriously can rest content with any *status quo*. There is a constant dynamic within scripture that forces us to examine our own circumstances with a critical and constructive eye. This is as true for the religious and ecclesiastical as it is for the political and economic.

At the risk of caricaturing a highly complex state of affairs, let me try to sketch the ecclesiastical situation here in Ireland today. There seem to be two churches: the one, at the official and respectable level, makes pronouncements, has interdenominational meetings, is very polite, and is rather ineffectual. The other, the 'grass roots church', does not make pronouncements, does not have interdenominational meetings, is not very polite to those outside its immediate catchment, and is effectual (but only on its own smallscale, personal and pietistic terms). At the official level, most leaders make a pass at ecumenism, believing it to be a good, if not very vital thing. Their joint pronouncements verge on the vacuous, treading skillfully but uninspiringly through a minefield of political, theological and emotional misunderstandings. Their very vacuity ensures that they are ignored. The grass roots majority has a deep seated and genuine prejudice against any such contacts, feeling them to be a 'betrayal of the Reformation' (or whatever). This, however, is an historically conditioned gut reaction, matured in our insecurity, the very antithesis of the biblical witness.

Neither church has made any serious attempt to do any practical theology. There is little or no attempt at any level (despite certain notable, but individually inspired, exceptions), to try to relate faith to real life, a situation that was specifically criticised in chapter 3, but which underlies the whole argument of this book. All the churches, by and large, have been content merely to mouth the formulae and slogans of previous generations, without even attempting to rephrase their content in today's language, or to relate them to today's world. There has been no attempt to try to challenge the powers that be with a biblical, prophetic, challenge. There has been no attempt at a specifically religious input into the political, social, or economic debates. There has been no attempt to ask questions, either of politicans or people, such as 'What does "salvation" mean for us in Northern Ireland today?', 'What does the biblical model of justice mean for us in Northern Ireland today?', 'What does Christ's witness to empathy and non-dominating power mean for us in Northern Ireland today?', 'What does "Shalom" mean for our society?', 'What does respect for persons and ideals and ideas mean for us?', 'What place do forgiveness and repentence have in our divided community?' The possible and important questions are endless. But they are rarely asked.

Christians in Northern Ireland today must ask these questions. They must grapple with them, difficult as they are, as individuals and as churches, at all levels. Theology of this importance cannot be left to the professionals or the synods: it must be done in the churches, in bible study groups, in the homes and bars and street corners of this land. We owe that much to our biblical faith. By making religion into a largely private affair, only occasionally butting incongruously into the public domain (and then with largely tangential issues such as Sunday sport), we have managed to emasculate the gospel and render it ineffective in the market place.

There are, of course, many reasons for this, and it is not my intention to analyse them. Perhaps, just to mention a few, it is because most people prefer to accept a comfortable and unchallenging religion 'on authority from above'; perhaps it is because we prefer to have our prejudices confirmed, rather than be forced to examine them; perhaps it is because we do not want controversy; perhaps it is part and parcel of the innate Irish pietistic tendency that has been manifested throughout the 1600 years of our Christian history. But, whatever the causes, it is a state of affairs that bible-inspired and Christ-loving Christians should not easily accept.

This book so far has been suggesting ways in which the churches and individual Christians can make a valid input into the political process. It has been very critical of much that passes for 'Protestantism' in the public arena in the hope that some will be awakened to the deep scriptural commitment to change. In other words, I refuse to accept that the churches should remain out of politics. I reject the traditional 'two cities' theology and ecclesiology, which allows faith to affect only private sin and private attitudes. I am calling for the current *status quo*, in which the relationship of the churches to the political sphere is practically non-existent, to be abandoned.

This is not a call for 'Christian power', but rather a call for a sensitive and prophetic Christian input into current debates and problems. The churches have for too long fought shy of 'political' comment, for fear of losing members. There is a real danger that such input will be understood wrongly, as a claim on power and influence. It needs to be offered humbly, in the spirit of Christ, as a genuine contribution towards the building up of a new society, for the benefit of all.

This is, of course, very risky, when so many are content with a narrow, exclusivist interpretation of their favourite texts, or regard the gospel, uncritically, as an *imprimatur* for a Protestant ascendancy. There are many who will be content to misinterpret the book of Revelation as a condemnation of the Church of Rome, and then use that as a justification for a thinly disguised sectarianism. Yet I have confidence enough in the power of God, and in the basic integrity of our people, to feel that the risk is worth taking. The contradictions between the deepest biblical witness, and so much of our so-called 'Protestant' ranting, need to be exposed for the sake both of the Province and of the gospel itself.

A realistic Christian input into the political and peacemaking process depends on the Christian churches and denominations getting their own houses in order. The syncopated dissonance of Christian voices today, the vitriol that is still traded, most especially in the letters columns of local and church newspapers, the crass unwillingness even to want to understand, the refusal to accept that others have changed – all these need to be tackled internally by the Christian churches. It is a process of purification that will never be over; it is a process that needs to go on in parallel to the wider political witness. It is the pariah process of ecumenism.

Texts such as, 'Do not try to work together as equals with unbelievers, for it cannot be done. How can right and wrong be partners? How can light and darkness live together? How can Christ and the Devil agree?' (2 Cor 6:14-15), are often used as cannon fodder in the war against ecumenism. But this is a typical case of taking texts out of context: the argument here in Paul is against cooperation with non-Christians. In the very same passage he proclaims, 'So then, let us purify ourselves from everything that makes body and soul unclean' (2 Cor 7:1) i.e. jealousy, party spirit, emnity (Gal 5:20) and self-righteousness (Mt 22:1-28; Lk 18:9-14). The anti-ecumenical attitude all too often smacks of the 'I'm right; you're wrong' sort of self-righteousness that typified the worst among the Pharisees.

Some will quote passages like Titus 3:10-11: 'Give at least two warnings to the person who causes divisions, and then have nothing more to do with him. You know that such a person is corrupt, and his sins prove that he is wrong.' But to use this (or any other such text) as an excuse for exclusivism, is to be on very shaky ground. Historically, it is easier to prove that it is we Protestants who caused the divisions. And today is it not we Protestants who are more likely to set up our own denomination, and thus prove ourselves to be the divisive ones? In Northern Ireland today all have cooperated (if that is the right word!), wittingly or unwittingly, in the causing and perpetuating of our divisions. That fact should lead us to repentence, not exclusivism.

There are New Testament passages that suggest that 'heretics' should be expelled from communion. Jezebel, who called herself a messenger of God, was misleading the Christians at Thyatira, and is threatened with death in punishment (Rev 2:20ff); the Christians at Pergamum, who were following the teachings of a certain Balaam and the Nicolaitans, are similarly threatened with 'the sword that comes out of my mouth' (Rev 2:14-16). But the teachings of these people were of a totally different kind from those put forward by the Roman Catholic Church today, and we should not, in fairness to the text, make any such simple equation. These teachers encouraged their followers to indulge in pagan rites, sexual orgies (frequently one and the same thing) and eat food offered to idols. They were teachers who encouraged an extreme form of antinomianism, a pseudo-freedom in which Christians were allowed to do anything. This is a far cry from the largely theological differences that divide the churches today.

The prevailing attitude to such divisions is well expressed by Paul:

> When one of you says, 'I follow Paul,', and another, 'I follow Apollos', aren't you acting like worldly people? After all, who is Apollos? And who is Paul? We are simply God's servants, by whom you were led to believe. Each one of us has done the work which the Lord gave him to do: I planted the seed, Apollos watered the plant, but it was God who made the plant grow. The one who plants and the one who waters really do not matter. It is God who matters, because he makes the plant grow. There is no difference between the man who plants and the man who waters; God will reward each one according to the work he has done. For we are partners working together for God, and you are God's field. (1 Cor 3:4-9)

If we were to substitute 'Roman Catholicism' for Apollos, and 'Presbyterianism' (or whatever) for Paul, I do not feel that we would be stretching Paul's point. The Roman Catholic and Protestant Churches are God's imperfect servants, by whom we were led to believe. Imperfect belief, perhaps, yet none the less belief, and precious in the eyes of God.

Elsewhere Paul refers to God's wisdom 'in all its different forms' (Eph 3:10). And in Philippians, having criticised some for preaching Christ from the wrong motives, he concludes with the startling statement: 'It does not matter! I am happy about it just so Christ is preached in every way possible, whether from wrong or right motives.' (Phil 1:18) Even in 1 Cor 11:18-19, where he strongly criticises the Corinthians for their party spirit, and where he does most certainly accuse one side of being wrong, he does not seem overconcerned with the fact of division. It is the negative attitudes that lie behind their party spirit that cause him most concern.

The New Testament does have some harsh things to say about false teachers (e.g. 2 Pet 2; Tis 1:10ff), but its main criticism is not for those who teach false doctrines. Rather, the strong attack is against those who preach a compromise with the values of a pagan society (surely a continuing and all-too-often ignored challenge for us in our hypermaterialistic society), and for those who 'deny the master who redeemed them' (2 Pet 2:1), and those who deny that 'Jesus Christ came as a human being' (1 Jn 4:2). Since the Roman Catholic Church today does none of these things, and does not encourage idolatry, sexual immorality or blatant compromise with the world (any more, that is, than we Protestants!), we can hardly refuse to accept them as fellow Christians.

The New Testament is concerned, rather, with the way in which our faith is expressed in action. The New Testament writers are more concerned with the way in which we live, than in the exact details of what we believe. The implication is that a true faith can be seen in the sort of people we become as a result of it. The creeds which mainstream Protestants share with the Roman Catholics are parameters outlining the limits of theological adventure: they are not straightjackets.

Here the Christian writers are building on the Old Testament prophets, who had no time for mere forms, if those forms were accompanied by injustice and oppression (e.g. Is 1; Amos 5; Hos 6; Mic 6; Ps 40). Christ himself preached a very works-centred idea of the judgement day: 'Not everyone who calls me "Lord, Lord," will enter the Kingdom of heaven, but only those who do what my Father in heaven wants them to do.' (Mt 7:21; cf. Mt 5:20; Ps 60:12) When talking about false prophets, Our Lord does not give us a dogmatic canon against which to measure their teaching, but says rather 'You will know them by what they do.' (Mt 7:16) Also in the Sermon on the Mount, Christ reflects on the Old Testament law in these words: 'Do for others what you want them to do for you: for this is the meaning of the Law of Moses and of the teachings of the Prophets.' (Mt 7:12) In his parable of the final judgement, the right-eous are judged righteous by what they did, and not by what they believed (Mt 25:31-46; cf. Job 34:11; Jer 17:10; 2 Tim 4:14; Rev 2:23). And referring elsewhere to the same last judgement, he says 'For the Son of Man is about to come in the glory of his Father with his angels, and then he will reward each one according to his deeds.' (Mt 16:27)

This emphasis is not confined solely to the gospel as recorded by St Matthew. Paul, who is often one-sidedly cited as the apostle of 'justification by faith alone', is equally capable of statements such as 'For it is not by hearing the law that people are put right with God, but by doing what the law commands.' (Rom 2:13; cf. Rom 2:6; 2 Cor 5:10; Jas 1:22-25) The writer of 1 Timothy refers to 'lawbreakers and criminals ... the godless and the sinful ... those who are not religious or spiritual ... those who kill their fathers or mothers ... murderers ... the immoral ... sexual perverts ... kidnappers ... those who lie and give false testimony or who do *anything else contrary to sound doctrine.*' (1 Tim 1:9-10) The implication is that sound doctrine is a good moral life not a set of dogmatic propositions. This is borne out later in the same book, where we are told that 'if anyone does not take care of his relatives, especially the members of his own family, he has denied the faith and is worse than an unbeliever.' (1 Tim 5:8) Or, in Titus, 'They claim to know God, but their actions deny it.' (Tit 1:16) Indeed, in the whole of Titus 'sound doctrine' (2:1) is defined in terms of behaviour, not in terms of the acceptance of certain propositions about the faith.

I am not seeking to enter into the argument concerning justification by faith, but merely to point out that the New Testament is more concerned with the ethical fruits of faith than with the detailed dogmatic content of that faith. To accept that 'Jesus Christ is Lord' is (as the World Council of Churches recognises) enough, at least to start with. The validity of that faith is either affirmed or denied by the sort of life lived by the one who holds it. This makes judgement very difficult (if it is to be encouraged at all – Mt 7:1). The bias seems to be in favour of *orthopraxy* (right action), and not *orthodoxy* (right belief).

In Northern Ireland this could easily be misinterpreted. A popular phrase amongst Protestants here is 'good living', which means basically that a person doesn't smoke or drink or go with bad women. It is taken as a sure sign that one is 'saved'. It is a kind of orthopraxy, but an othopraxy that has gone off the rails.

The other day someone was telling me of a conversation they had had. It went something like this:

'What Church do you belong to?'

'The Church of Ireland.'

'Oh!' ... followed by a long pause. 'Is your minister a Christian?'

'Yes, of course.'

'Well, does he drink?'

'I think so – the odd beer now and then.'

'Well then,' there was something half way between relief and triumph in yer man's voice, 'he's not a Christian.'

That attitude is common, and it fairly annoys me. I see no point in arguing the drink question Scripture is clear enough that Jesus turned the water into wine (Jn 2:1-11), that he enjoyed a drink (Lk 5:30), and that he was dismissed by his enemies as a 'glutton and a winebibber' (Mt 11:19). What I do want to point out is the falsity of a narrowly defined orthopraxy that says that a person is not a Christian unless she does, thinks and says exactly what a given speaker or tradition thinks she should do, think or say. Orthopraxy (ghastly word, but useful!) is expressed more in terms of attitudes that underlie actions, a caring looking outward, such as we have been trying to define in this chapter and the one before. It should not be confused with a petty list of 'Thou shalt not's.

This is, of course, a big over-simplification, but I hope that, by trying to emphasise elements of the New Testament witness that are often ignored here in Northern Ireland, I can do something to redress the imbalance in our Protestant thinking. Things are not as clear cut as many of us would like. There are huge grey areas: the rest of this chapter will seek to show how it is vital for us to seek respectful and non-condemnatory dialogue with members of all churches. We owe it to our biblical faith.

Let me begin here by listing three statements that we should take very seriously in any ecumenical or inter-church debate:

No one can confess 'Jesus is Lord' unless he is guided by the Holy Spirit. (1 Cor 12:3)

Anyone who acknowledges that Jesus Christ came as a human being has the Spirit that comes from God. (1 Jn 4:2)

If anyone declares that Jesus is the Son of God, he lives in union with God and God lives in union with him. (1 Jn 4:15; cf. 2:22-23)

On this yardstick, if on no other, we have a duty to regard Roman Catholics as fellow Christians. They say the same creed and accept the same scriptures (with a few extra books that the Protestant Churches, following Jerome, rejected at the Reformation). They admit that Jesus is Lord, that he comes from God, and that he is the Son of God. This is enough to call a foundational agreeement on doctrinal essentials. We should not be blinded to this by the obvious, but ultimately less fundamental, doctrinal disagreements, the importance of which are, anyway, lessened by our emphasis earlier in the chapter on orthopraxis over and above orthodoxy.

I have said 'they accept the same scriptures'. This needs to be explained to many Protestants who seem to believe that Roman Catholics are not allowed to read the Bible. But, especially since Vatican II, which specifically declared that 'access to sacred scripture ought to be wide open to the Christian faithful' (*Dei Verbum* 22), this is not true. The *Dogmatic Constitution on Divine Revelation* states, among other things, that 'we must acknowledge that the books of scripture, firmly, faithfully and without error, teach that which God, for the sake of our salvation, wished to see confided to the sacred scripture.' (*Dei Verbum* 11); the church 'has always regarded, and continues to regard the scriptures, taken together with sacred tradition, as the supreme rule of her faith. For, since they are inspired by God and committed to writing once for all time, they present God's own word in unalterable form ... it follows that all the preaching of the church, as indeed of the entire Christian religion, should be nourished and ruled by sacred scripture.' (*ibid* 21)

To take an example from closer to home, Bishop Cahal Daly in his 'Message to his People' in Down and Connor on 11 May, 1986, says the following: 'The word in which we believe and by which we try to live is the word of God, made flesh in Jesus Christ, the word entrusted to the church in holy scripture. Our most essential Christian reading is the Bible. Every Catholic home should possess a Bible. Every family should read it. It would be impressive and natural, indeed, to find the Bible in an honoured place in every Catholic home, placed open perhaps on a table or a stand, with a light burning occasionally before it.'

The impact of these almost fundamentalist statements is rather dulled for many Protestants by the addition of the words 'taken together with sacred tradition'. There is, obviously, much in the Roman Catholic tradition that we Protestants find hard to swallow, but I do not think that the principal is so very far removed from that which we Protestants follow in practice. Each Protestant denomination has tended to make its own tradition of biblical interpretation the infallible yardstick of doctrine. The Roman Catholics would maintain with us that nothing in the tradition should be seen to contradict the Bible. But they would also maintain that those doctrines to which we object, although not actually to be found within the pages of scripture, are in fact logical and legitimate developments of it. We may disagree, but our mutual regard for scripture should not be diminished by such disagreements.

So, starting from a shared worship of God, Father, Son and Holy Spirit, from a shared love of Christ, from a shared respect for holy scripture, and a shared will to be effective witnesses to Christ in our world today, we must seek Christian harmony. I use this word instead of *unity*, since the latter implies a rigidity and inflexibility that is not only unbiblical, but also totally unrealistic. Of course the Bible does use the word *unity* (e.g. Eph 4:3,13) but never in the straightjacket sense. Other than in Ephesians, the word is only used once, and then (in the *Good News Bible* at least) is translated as *harmony*:

How wonderful it is, how pleasant,

for God's people to dwell together in harmony! (Ps 133:1)

Harmony is a pleasant image, for it is more enriching than mere monotonal unity; harmony allows different notes to work together to create a complex and more interesting unity, such as was seen among the disciples themselves. Christ prayed that they might be one (Jn 17:21), and they became one, despite their divergent political outlooks (see Chapter 2). They travelled the known world as evangelists, founding different churches, with different emphases. Yet they were pulling in the same direction, they were working in harmony. They were not clones of each other, mouthing the same formulae: they were individuals who in their individual richness responded to Christ with a rich diversity, part of which is integral to the Christian inheritance today (as can be seen in the differences between John and the other three gospels). That sort of harmony is, I believe, the necessary goal of the ecumenical movement, not least in Northern Ireland, where it is so complicated by other, non-theological factors.

If we speak the truth to each other in love (Eph 4:5), instead of shouting our 'truths' and refusing to listen or hear tell of any other 'truth', there is a chance that we might begin to learn something from each other. If we have the courage to abandon the silly pretence that 'our side' has a monopoly of truth, there is a chance that we might begin to have the riches of our own tradition enriched from the 'other side'. If we can muster the courage to accept that we might be wrong (and surely that assumption is implicit in the whole idea of faith in contra-distinction to knowledge), then there is a chance that a harmony might break out between our various church traditions. Not a total agreement, but the harmony that grows out of the recognition that God himself is truer than our formulations of his greatness are ever likely to be. For this to be acheived there is a crying need to listen. We are not good at that here in Northern Ireland. Those who refuse to listen are masking their own uncertainty and fear behind a belligerency that does little service to the gospel of Christ.

This point deserves to be laboured a little. Most Protestants and all Roman Catholics here in Northern Ireland recognise that there is one God and one Saviour, only one mediator between God and man (cf. 1 Tim 2:5). Both recognise 'one Lord, one Faith, one Baptism' (Eph 4:45). Yet the average Protestant is more scared of the vague 'Roman' threat than he is of the far more unorthodox pre-millenial dispensationalism of the Brethren or the non-trinitarianism of the

Unitarians. I am not advocating that we suddenly replace Rome with the Brethren in our scarlet woman theologies. I am rather pointing out that our history here in Northern Ireland has warped our theological judgement. All our churches have different theological emphases, even within themselves. There is no such thing as 'The Protestant Faith' in Northern Ireland, but instead there is a huge diversity. It is plainly ridiculous to harp on the Roman Catholic 'heresies' and ignore those of our Protestant brethren.

We Ulster Protestants have Rome on the brain, largely for historical reasons. Even a cursory reading of Irish history since the landing of Strongbow near Waterford in August 1169 will reveal a considerable interaction between tribal, political and religious factors. Especially since the Act of Union in 1801, the Protestant = pro-British = anti-Roman Catholic equation has been very strong. Christians need to be aware of that and, difficult though the process may be, they need to try to separate the politicial and tribal animosities from the more rational and theological differences. That is a tall order. As Christians we need to try to examine our theological differences for what they are, and not merely for what our other differences have made them appear to be. Then, as Christians, we need to apply our newly awakened, biblically inspired and practical theological understanding to these other areas.

My discussion, in Chapter 4, of the theological lessons that I learned in Papua New Guinea is especially relevant to my thesis here. Maybe I jumped the gun by discussing that experience where I did, since for me the primary message of my time in that country was theological. The experience of trying to live an alien theology was both hard and very valuable: to be able to appreciate that others could be met by God along a road that held no attractions for me was not a comforting message. It is far more comforting to feel that 'I alone am right'; it is far more reassuring to feel that the path I follow is the only real path. But it isn't right: and here in Northern Ireland, such are the attitudes upon which our extremists thrive.

The Cornerstone Community, of which I am a member, has tried during its short life to live out the ecumenical ideal in a small way. We are united by a shared love for Christ and our people, and have really sought to understand our various ways of thinking. We have long since ceased to pretend that we have no differences, but through open discussion we have sought to understand the rationale and integrity behind those differences. This has not always been easy, especially during times of high communal tension, when political and emotional factors have threatened to come between us. Some of our most valuable times have occured when we have just sat and listened to each other explaining our various beliefs on The Holy Communion, or Authority. Even the supposedly well educated among us were devastated by the level of our ignorance. Now that ignorance is being removed, we find that we are far closer to each other in faith, although perhaps not in dogma.

On one interesting occasion, a group of us went to a Novena at Holy Trinity Church in Turf Lodge. None of us Protestants felt happy with the theology that lay behind some of what went on, but none of us could deny that this was a real experience for those who took part, and that the prayers offered were deep and genuine. As our resident octogenarian Methodist said to me afterwards, 'I can't condemn this now.'

We need now to discuss this experience in the light of the biblical witness. Was it a real experience? Have I interpreted it correctly? Does God really call us to ecumenism? And if so, of what sort?

Paul, as we have already mentioned, refers to God's wisdom 'in all its different forms' (Eph 3:10). That is, at least, suggestive of diversity, of a pluriformity of witness. Elsewhere (1 Cor 12:12-31) he makes an extended discussion on the nature of the church as a 'body with many parts'. Although the main thrust of his argument is to encourage the Corinthian Christians to think through the diversity of rôles within their own church community, what he says can be legitimately applied to the wider ecumenical (literally: whole wide world) sphere.

> In the same way all of us, whether Jews (? Protestants/ Unionists/Scots-Irish) or Gentiles (? Roman Catholics/Republicans/ Celts), whether slave (? working class) or free (? middle class) have been baptised into the one body by the same Spirit, and we have all been given the one Spirit to drink. (1 Cor 12:13)

In verse 15 he says:

> If the foot were to say, 'Because I am not a hand I don't belong to the body', that would not keep it from being a part of the body ... (v. 18) As it is, God put every part in the body just as he wanted it to be ! (1 Cor 12:15-18)

It is not stretching Paul's meaning to continue the argument along these lines: if the Free Presbyterians were to say to the Church of Ireland 'Because you are not a Free Presbyterian, you don't belong to the body', that would not keep the Church of Ireland from being part of the body.

The same metaphor is introduced, although in a less expanded form, in Romans:

> We have many parts in the one body, and all these parts have
> different functions. In the same way, although we are many, we
> are one body in union with Christ, and are all joined to each
> other as different parts of one body. (Rom 12:45)

Each of our churches has a different gift: the Presbyterians a gift of
Scriptural knowledge; the Baptists the gift of regenerative preaching; the Roman Catholics the gifts of contemplative prayer and
sacramental worship; the Church of Ireland the gift of liturgical
worship and pastoral care; the Methodists the gift of hymn singing;
the Salvation Army the gift of good works; the Quakers the gift of
peacemaking, and so on. But none of us is perfect, and all our gifts
can be turned into something stolid and unexciting. But we are all
children of God, with our good and bad points, with our merits and
faults, with our truths and falsehoods. To recognise that we all have
different gifts and different functions in God's plan, that we are all
different parts of the same body and not competing bodies; to
recognise that we all have a mixture of good and bad, both as individuals and as institutions – that is a way forward.

We are parts of the same body; or, to use more theological language, we are all parts of the one church. Our Lord's words, in a different context, are very apposite here: 'Any country that divides
itself into groups which fight each other will not last very long. And
any town or family that divides itself into groups which fight each
other will fall apart.' (Mt 12:25) Are we not doing precisely that to
the church? Aren't our divisions, bitter as they are, a fatal flaw in
our shared witness to the world ? Our divisions threaten the very
existence of the church, and undermine any pretence of effective
witness. To put it mildly, the situation is a tragedy.

No doubt many readers, if they have survived this far, will be
wanting to protest: What about the Pope? What about Mary? What
about confession? What about the Mass? Good – these questions
need to be discussed, and not swept under the carpet. It is a phoney
ecumenism that pretends that differences don't exist. My concern in
this book is not to examine the rights and wrongs of such differences, but to clear the ground so that they can be discussed in an
atmosphere of mutual love and respect, in the recognition that we
are all searching, feebly and inadequately, to understand the length
and breadth and height of the love of God (Eph 3:18). The prevailing atmosphere of acrimony, self-righteousness and accusation cannot get us anywhere.

Each one of us feels a little hurt when someone debunks our
deepest convictions. When I hear of some Protestants saying that

you can't be a Christian and a member of the Church of Ireland (to say nothing of the Roman Catholic Church!), I feel a little hurt. I feel that my relationship with Christ and his with me has been misunderstood. Therefore, in order to avoid returning that hurt, I go out of my way not to suggest the same thing of the Free Presbyterian or Baptist who said that of me. I can appreciate that they have come to Christ, but I cannot follow their path, which I find very unattractive. I only wish that they could do the same for me and recognise that I too have been with Christ and have been saved and changed by him, despite the weird path that I have trod. 'Do for others what you want them to do for you.' (Mt 7:12) Exclusivity has no part in Christian living.

Those who look to the Old Testament as their prime authority, can of course find much that is very exclusive in matters religious and tribal, where the command 'worship no God but me' (Ex 20:3) is taken to rather extreme conclusions. In Deuteronomy, for instance, we read:

> When the Lord your God places these people in your power and you defeat them, you must put them all to death. Do not make an alliance with them, or show them any mercy. Do not marry any of them, and do not let your children marry any of them, because then they would lead your children away from the Lord to worship other gods. (Deut 7:2-4a)

This was done: all the inhabitants of Jericho, saving only Rahab and her family, were put to the sword (Josh 6:21). The same happened to the inhabitants of Ai (Josh 8:24), Debir (Josh 10:39), Hazor (Josh 11:10-11) and many other cities. King Saul was rejected as King of Israel because he spared the lives of some of his enemies (1 Sam 15:17-23). Elijah massacred the prophets of Baal (1 Kgs 18), and Ezra persuaded the people to divorce all their foreign wives (Ez 10), on the basis that they, like Jezebel, might lead their husbands astray.

The examples could be multiplied: but it is more important for our purpose to examine the less obvious, but significant, protest against such total exclusivity. The book of Jonah is a fine moral tale, relating how the prophet Jonah was taught a lesson: God cares for foreign peoples, even the hated Assyrians. Ruth is another beautiful story, that reminds its readers (who may just have divorced their foreign wives) that King David himself was the grandson of a foreign woman, and she of hated Moabite stock. While some zealots were trying to refuse foreigners the right of entry into the family of Israel, narrowly interpreting membership of God's people in racial terms, Isaiah said 'I will bring you (Gentiles) to Zion, my sacred hill,

give you joy in my house of prayer, and accept the sacrifices you
offer on my altar. My Temple will be called a house of prayer for all
of the nations.' (Is 57:7)

Indeed, there are parts of the Bible that strongly suggest that
even pagans worship God better than the so-called 'religious' Jew
or Christian: 'People from one end of the world to the other honour
me. Everywhere they burn incense to me and offer acceptable sacrifices. All of them honour me! But you dishonour me...' (Mal 1:11-
12). This was written long before anyone outside the Middle East
had had the opportunity to hear of the Lord God of Israel: it should
jolt us out of our exclusiveness and remind us that God judges by
different standards. Maybe there are parallels here with the Hindu
saying 'Even those who in faith worship other gods, because of
their love they worship me.' (*Bhagavad Gita* 9:23) There is biblical
justification (even if it is only part of a minority tradition within the
scriptural traditions) for saying that even those who are 'wrong'
could, in the eyes of God, be more acceptable to him than we ourselves. Let that thought humble us.

Perhaps even more significant are those instances in which the
Old Testament borrows from other traditions. Psalm 19:16 seems to
be an adaptation of a Canaanite hymn to the Sun; Prov 22:17-23:14
are modelled on the Egyptian 30 Chapters of Amenemopet; Prov
16:18 is paralleled exactly in the Egyptian Papyrus Insinger; there
are at least eight echoes of the Mesopotamian Words of Ahikar in
the book of Proverbs. Even the religious centre of Jerusalem, incor-
porated late into Israel (2 Sam 5:6-10) was originally a Canaanite
centre of worship, where the Canaanite God El 'Elyon was worshipped (Gen 14:17-20). Many of the El 'Elyon traditions were
absorbed into the temple cult: the name El 'Elyon (Most High God)
was adopted itself after Jerusalem had become the political and religious centre of the nation, and then mainly in the Psalms: in other
words, it remained primarily a 'Jerusalem' name for the God of
Israel. (e.g. 2 Sam 22:14; Ps 7:17; 46:4; 91:9 etc.) This suggests, at the
very least, that the people of Jerusalem adopted the name of the
Canaanite High God as a suitable additional name for their God.
(The only apparent exceptions to this, Num 24:16 and Deut 32:89,
were written down fairly late in Israel's history, by which time the
name El 'Elyon had become a familiar part of Israel's vocabulary.)
And doubtless there are many other such borrowings that we will
never be able to trace, given the limited state of our knowledge of
ancient Near Eastern religion.

I do not believe that these borrowings amount to syncretism. I believe rather that they happened because some pious Jew read them and said to himself: 'Yes, that is also true of the Lord my God. I can hear his voice there.' The Jewish people, as the above examples show, could be horribly exclusive and inward looking; but they could also rebel against such attitudes, and in the name of the same faith that supported that xenophobia. Both such attitudes are found in the pages of the Bible. Some, no doubt, would have vehemently condemned those who read Egyptian and Mesopotamian religious works. Yet, in their reading, they found many good things. They were open to the truth, even from the 'enemy'. That kind of openness needs to be cultivated in Northern Ireland today.

It has been said that an exclusive love for Christ lifts us out of our exclusiveness into his all-inclusive love. If it doesn't, the fault lies with us, and not with him. The God who makes his sun to shine on both the good and the evil (Mt 5:45) loves both the good and the evil: he came to summons the sinners to the Kingdom (Mk 2:17). The God who has, in Christ, accepted us freely and unconditionally (Rom 5:17; Eph 5:2) demands that we must accept our fellow Christians freely and unconditionally as well, even if we regard them as mistaken on important issues.

Of course, this problem is not narrowly religious. In Northern Ireland it is intimately bound up with political and tribal emotions. I have already argued that we Christians need to try and disentangle the theological issues from the historical and the tribal. But things go far deeper than that. We have all allowed ourselves to be seduced by a false picture of God, which we have then projected onto society. Deep down we have a rather patriarchal, authoritarian view of God. We have interpreted the concepts of holiness and power in terms of remoteness, otherness and directive, non-consultative domination. God is God, we have reasoned; he has unlimited power; he says, and we obey; he is judge, condemning us to hell unless we tow the line. God is a God to be feared (in a negative modern sense, rather than in the biblical sence of respect); rarely is he seen as a God to be loved. He is seen as the judge, not as the Father running out to meet his prodigal child (Lk 15:50).

We have unconsciously projected that model onto society. The Northern Irish family has in the past often been very patriarchal, with the man as boss, to be obeyed without question. The civil authorities have, at least in the eyes of the Protestant community, been vested with a similar unchallenged authority (although, like the family model, that particular belief is fast breaking down). Our concept of society has reflected our rigid, authoritarian concept of

God. If we allowed our picture of God to mellow under the influence of Christ and his gospel, then our society would mellow and become more tolerant too. The whole task of reconciliation, at all levels, would become far easier. Christians have an uphill task: the Protestant community is now largely secularised, with no concept of God at all. As God has disintegrated, so has society.

This image of God is just that: an image. We have worshipped the image rather than the reality, and have thereby become guilty of idolatry. We have further compounded this by saying, in effect, that we will only accept our neighbours if they accept our image of God, our interpretation of truth. The Council of Trent said just the same (*Injunctum nobis*, Nov. 1564). Both Protestant and Roman Catholic have become guilty, not just of idolising God, but of idolising their own traditions. Both, at different times in their history, have chosen to mask their own sense of insecurity behind the idols of dogmatism that true religion just does not permit. Thankfully, the ecumenical movement is beginning to de-idolise us.

Protestants always accuse Roman Catholics of worshipping idols. But this is naïve. As the second Council of Nicaea (717) made clear, images are not worshipped, but only used so that, through them, worshippers might 'be aroused to recollect the originals and to long after them.' Statues are excellent *aides memoire*, that can keep our mind from wandering during prayer. We look at a crucifix and are reminded of Our Lord's passion and resurrection; we look at a statue of the Virgin and Child, and are drawn to Bethlehem and the first Christmas. St Louise-Marie Guignon de Montfort, the man who, more than any other, systematised and popularised what we Protestants would regard as 'mariolatry' noted that 'Jesus, our Saviour, true God and true man, must be the ultimate end of all other devotions; otherwise they are false and misleading.' (From his *True Devotion of the Blessed Virgin*, quoted in Saward, *Perfect Folds*, page 191). Obviously such an approach has its dangers, and can degenerate into genuine idolatry. But the same can happen to a Protestant over-emphasis on the Bible. The open Bible, the written word, has all too often become the centre of faith at the expense of the word made flesh. (Jn 1:14) We have replaced the living Christ with inanimate word. The Bible is of value only if we go through it to the God who is revealed in its pages: statues are only of value if we go behind them to the Lord Jesus Christ they are intended to lead us to.

Both our traditions have fallen into idolatry in different ways. In fact, we have gone further, and have tended to idolise the traditions themselves by confusing our *interpretation* of truth with truth itself. We have all too often elevated our definitions to the level of infallible truth, when in fact the only infallibility lies in him whom we are attempting to define. We have all too often acted as though our way of doing things were the only proper one, as though our form of worship were the only one acceptable to God. By doing this, we have obscured the Lord we thought we were serving.

We are judging ourselves. 'The light has come into the world, but people love darkness rather than light.' (Jn 3:19) We have grown to love our own theses better than Christ, and have remained in darkness as a result. But Christ has 'come into the world as light, so that everyone who believes in (him) should not remain in darkness.' (Jn 12:46) He has come that we might be free (Jn 8:36; Rom 8:2; 1 Cor 7:22). But we have all bonded ourselves to the slavery of our own traditions; we have become involved in an idolatry of whose existence we are hardly aware. This goes for all religious traditions in Northern Ireland and all need to come together to Christ, the head, and seek to know him better. Faced with our own shortcomings, are we not being a bit hypocritical in always emphasising the supposed failings and errors of the 'other side'? (Mt 7:15)

Or take holy scripture, which has only recently been granted its rightful place in the Roman Catholic tradition (see above). We Protestants often insist on 'sola scriptura' (only scripture), and damn Rome for her 'additions' or developments. But that condemnation is hardly convincing when there are literally dozens of little churches, all claiming to be faithful to holy scripture, yet all with vastly differing theologies, church orders, and practices. As we have already seen, it is hardly even scripture that is being idolised, but our own divergent interpretations of it, raised to a level of infallibility that would amuse even Pope Pius IX. Besides, Christ himself, although highly respectful of scripture, does leave the door open to further developments and further revelation: 'When, however, the Spirit comes, who reveals the truth about God, he will lead you into all truth...'(Jn 16:13) The Protestant, who is tempted to run to the Bible for cover when confronted with Roman Catholic 'innovations', is not on as sure ground as he might have thought. We need a humility, we need to search the scriptures (Jn 5:39), not for cannon fodder in our war of words, but for Christ himself. After all, it is not scripture or tradition, but Christ who is the object and goal of our faith.

In this chapter I have tried to lay the foundations for ecumenical relations in Northern Ireland by emphasising what we have in common. I have also questioned, from within, some of our own Protestant securities, in the hope that much that is obstructive and irrelevant can be cleared from the ground, and that we will then be better able to enter that new ecumenical relationship with humility, and less cock-sureness. We need to put into practice the model of forgiveness that was outlined in the political context of the last chapter. For we do need to forgive: to forgive much wilful ignorance; to forgive much ecclesiastical imperialism; to forgive much calumny; and to forgive the fear and mistrust with which we have been treated for so long. At the same time we must accept that we, too, need to be forgiven for very similar offences. That needs a little less Rambo, and a little more Christ.

Our Rambo approach to interchurch affairs has ignored a fundamental truth of the Reformation: *semper reformanda* (always being reformed). We betray the Reformers so long as we remain in their rut. The Reformation was seeking to return to roots, and as our knowledge of those roots is expanded by chance discovery (like the discovery of the *Didache* in 1875) and by scholarship, so our perception of how we can best act out our Reformation principals will also change. We must be open to the possibility, indeed the desirability, of change, always striving upwards and forward to new expressions of the new life in Christ. But we in Ulster are far from that. We have retreated into our laagers, and repeated out-of-date answers to out-of-date questions. Let us be open to the future.

God is decreeing to begin some new and great period in his church, even to the reforming of the Reformation itself. (John Milton, *Areopogitica*, 1644).

We in Northern Ireland should be playing our part in that.

Conclusion

'We will smash the Anglo-Irish Agreement; but more important, let us build a new united Ulster for all our people.' (Poster on lamp-post on the Springmartin Road, Belfast, Spring 1986)

Although I do not like the word 'smash', I can identify with this slogan – so much more constructive than the incessant 'No's of recent years. The positive note struck by the second half of the sentence is in tune with much of what I have been saying in the earlier chapters of this book. But the fact that I saw this poster only once, and that it has since been drowned out by 'Ulster says No', or 'Ulster still says No', only goes to show that the negative and destructive side of so much Ulster unionism was very much in the ascendant then, and is still in the ascendant today.

A walk down Belfast's Shankill Road and some of its back streets in June 1986 revealed shop windows plastered with 'Ulster says No', on posters, on stickers, on caps, scarves and teeshirts. It revealed heraldic wall art to the UDA (Ulster Defence Association), the UVF (Ulster Volunteer Force), the Shankill Road Defenders and King Billy. It revealed graffiti that could not rise above scrawled letters UFF (Ulster Freedom Figthters), PAF (Protestant Action Force) or statements such as 'Kill Fitzgerald Now'; 'Fuck Your Deal'; 'The RUC are Fitzgerald's Puppets'; 'Fitzgerald is a sick man'; 'RUC Scum – garda wee (*sic*) got your houses! Ha! Ha!'; 'Fuck Taigs'; it revealed a poster which, under the words 'Say No', advised the following: 'Ulster is fighting for its existence. Come forward to be trained to do your share. Every fit man owes this duty to himself and his country. ORGANISE NOW!' Although many (even most) of the Shankill folk would have been ashamed of much of this, they are crude expressions of much of what passes for unionist orthodoxy today. Our political representatives, on the whole, are more subtle in their phrasing: but their meaning is the same.

Too much of Ulster unionism has lost its way. It often appears to be totally negative. Is it, in its apparant unwillingness to be constructive, in danger of moving ever further away both from its own truest self and from the gospel of Jesus Christ? Is it also, because of its close identification with Ulster Protestantism, in danger of bringing Christian faith itself into disrepute? I recently heard of a Japanese Buddhist, interested in converting to Christianity, who drew back because of the effect that Northern Irish 'Christians' had on him. If Buddhist sects in Japan could live together, he reckoned that Buddhism was preferebale to Christianity.

This is one reason why I have argued on two fronts, the political and the religious. In Northern Ireland today we cannot divorce the two. Anyone who genuinely desires peace and justice in this land must seek them in both the political and religious spheres, at one and the same time. Even after the ceasefires, there is no real *shalom* in our land. So long as we Ulster Protestants refuse to respect or even hear the political and religious opinions of our Roman Catholic neighbours, there will be division and hatred in our land.

It is my belief that all this is totally antithetical to the gospel of Jesus Christ. Our present troubles are in no small measure caused by the refusal of Christians to take their faith seriously – in other words, by the refusal of Christians to be Christian. The brunt of my critique has been aimed at Protestants and unionists, not because they are any better or worse than Catholics and nationalists, but because I am (in Northern Irish terminology at least) a Protestant, and I have been nurtured in a broadly unionist ethos. As much blame lies with the 'other side' but it is not for me to offer a similar critique of the nationalist/Catholic community.

There is an old hymn, written in 1696, which runs:

Fear him, ye saints, and you will then
Have nothing else to fear ...

We in Ulster have been idolaters – we have not feared or respected God. One result of this has been that we have had a whole lot else to fear. Deep down we have feared the Gaelic people whom our ancestors dispossessed. We have feared their church and their political representatives. And since partition we have feared Dublin. Had we been fully focused on God, Father, Son and Holy Spirit, I am sure that all of these other fears would long ago have evaporated, and that we could by now be calling ourselves a Christian nation, living in the excitement of God's *shalom*.

We claim to be 'Protestants', reformed Christians who look to the Bible for inspiration and authority (however defined), yet our way of life over the last twenty-five years (not to mention the last sixty or six hundred) has been a sorry travesty of that very gospel. The fruits of the Spirit have not been apparent in our lives or in our attitudes. We have allowed our religion to become the uncritical servant of our unionism. Surely, had we truly been worshippers of the One God, our criticisms of government and society would have grown, not out of the narrow instinct of self-preservation, but out of a prophetic understanding of the needs and aspirations of *all* the people. Our unionism would have been inspired by a biblically-conditioned understanding of the will of God, and infected by the Spirit of him whom we claim to worship.

I have a vision of a Protestant people infected by that Spirit: a Protestant people open to the religion and personhood and expectation of others; a Protestant people who have grown out of xenophobia into the all-inclusive love of Christ; a Protestant people who have bravely stepped out in search of the truth, wherever that search may take them; a Protestant people who seek the unity of, and justice for, all our peoples, and are critically open to all possibilities; a Protestant people who are confident enough to be penitent about the past and optimistic about the futre. In short, I have a vision of the people of Ulster, united in love for God, and willing to serve him above all other; an Ulster in which the old ideologies have died away, and in which the Kingdom of God is allowed to grow, unhindered by our historically conditioned fears, hatreds and aspirations.